DAVID WEATHERLY
MONSTERS OF
BIG SKY COUNTRY
CRYPTIDS & LEGENDS
OF
MONTANA
FOREWORD BY JOHN LEMAY

Eerie Lights Publishing
Eerielightspublishing.com

DAVID WEATHERLY
MONSTERS OF
BIG SKY COUNTRY
CRYPTIDS & LEGENDS
OF
MONTANA
FOREWORD BY JOHN LEMAY

Based on interviews and research conducted by David Weatherly

ISBN: 978-1-945950-26-1 (Paperback)

Published by:

EERIE LIGHTS
Eerie Lights Publishing
Eerielightspublishing.com

Cover design: Sam Shearon
www.mister-sam.com

Editor: Jerry Hajewski

Book layout/design: SMAK
www.smakgraphics.com

Printed in the United States of America

Also by David Weatherly

Strange Intruders
Eerie Companions: A History of Haunted Dolls
Black Eyed Children

Silver State Monsters: Cryptids & Legends of Nevada
Copper State Monsters: Cryptids & Legends of Arizona
Monsters of the Last Frontier: Cryptids & Legends of Alaska
Monsters at the Crossroads: Cryptids & Legends of Indiana
Monsters of the Tar Heel State: Cryptids & Legends of North Carolina
Peach State Monsters: Cryptids & Legends of Georgia

The Haunted Series (co-authored with Ross Allison)
Haunted Toys
Haunted Ships & Lighthouses
Haunted Churches
Haunted Prisons

Shadow Chaser (co-authored with Sean Austin)
Shadow Chaser: The In-Between (co-authored with Sean Austin)

Paranormal Files: West Virginia

Wood Knocks: A Journal of Sasquatch Research
Volume One
Volume Two
Volume Three
Volume Four

Table of Contents

1
Foreword

5
Introduction

PART ONE:
The Shunka Warak'in

11
The Shunka Warak'in

15
What's in a Name?

21
The Taxidermy Trail

27
The Creature of McCone County

PART TWO:
Sasquatch in the Treasure State

35
Native Tales and Early Accounts

49
Bigfoot Through the Decades

PART THREE:
Water Monsters

101
Legends of Lakes and Rivers

105
Water Babies

109
The Flathead River and Flathead Lake

115
Flathead Lake Monster

121
Sightings

135
The Monster Today

PART FOUR:
Assorted Curiosities

141
A Horrible Monster

145
The Yellowstone Dinosaur

149
Giant Snakes

153
Weird Things in the Big Sky

157
Thunderbirds

165
Montana Mothman

167
Attack of the Bird Men

175
Living Lights

181
Little People of the Pryor Mountains

193
The Pedro Mountain Mummy

197
Modern Accounts of the Little People

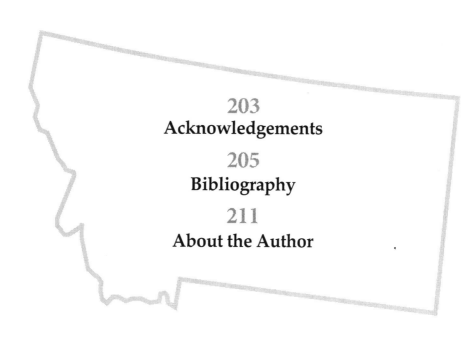

203
Acknowledgements

205
Bibliography

211
About the Author

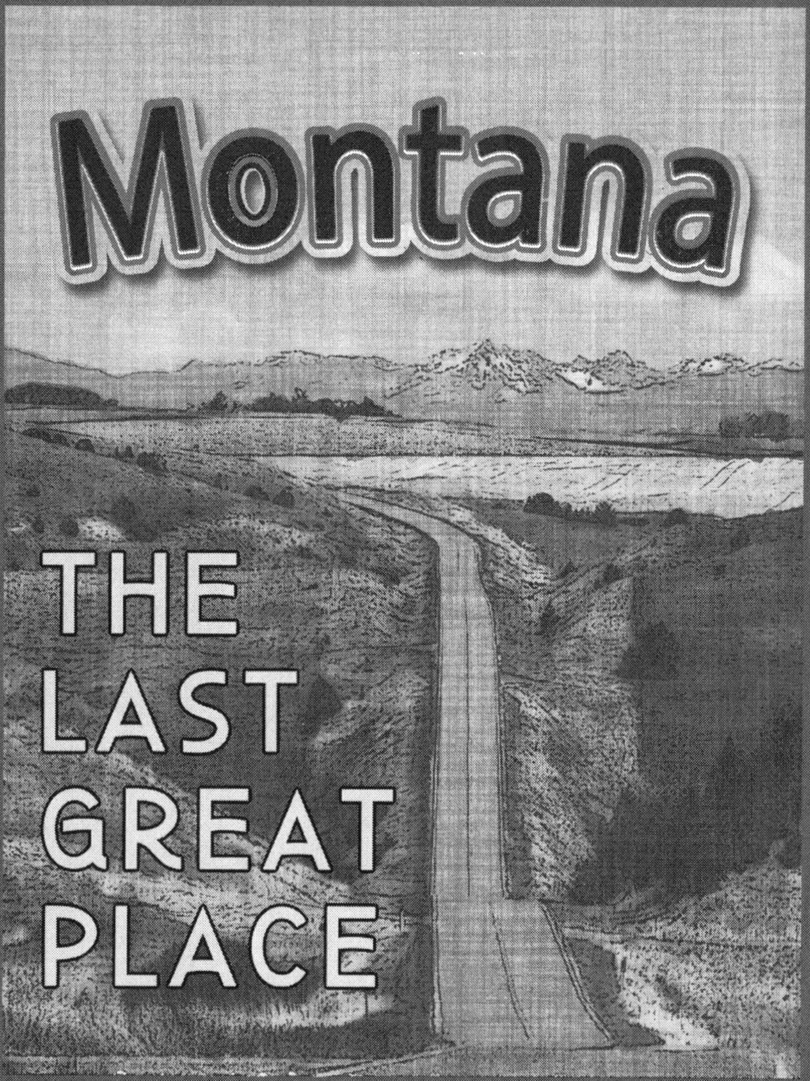
Montana
THE
LAST
GREAT
PLACE

Foreword

Hello, and I bid you welcome from Roswell, New Mexico, UFO Capital of the World and Land of Little Green Men!

I know, I know, you came here to read about the monsters of Montana, not the aliens of New Mexico. And so why am I writing this foreword? Well, there are two reasons for that. First of all, like you, I love cryptids, monsters, and mystery creatures not yet accepted by mainstream science. And why is it that I love monsters more than aliens? Probably it's because I grew up in a land where alien heads dotted the streetlights, and cardboard cutouts of them could be found on nearly every corner of Main Street; and like so many kids, I wasn't interested in what was right in front of me. I was interested in faraway monsters: Bigfoot, Nessie, Mokele-mbembe… the list could go on and on. In the mid-1990s I read every book I could find on cryptids and real-life monsters. As a kid I thought that monsters only existed in faraway places, like the jungle swamps of the Congo and the dreary depths of Loch Ness. As far as I could tell back then, and aside from Bigfoot, the United States of America was lacking in monsters when compared to the rest of the world. But, as my casual reading evolved into serious research as I got older, I learned that strange creatures are seen all across America. (There's even been a mini-dinosaur sighting here in Roswell!).

In his typical fashion, David has also turned up some truly strange Montana monsters outside of the usual Sasquatch and serpentine lake monsters. In addition to Bigfoot tales, you've got what might be the most comprehensive chapter ever written on the Shunka Warak'in, plus the Flathead Lake Monster. As a cryptid-enthusiast, you've probably heard of those. But, on the weirder spectrum of things you've probably never heard of before, you'll find tales of a Montana Mothman, an enchanted

Meganeura, and what sounded to me to be tiny pterodactyl-like aliens, just to name a few! So, as usual, you're in for a treat when it comes to well-known and lesser-known cryptids alike.

Anyhow, that's the first reason I was invited to write a foreword for David: I love monsters. The second reason I was asked to write this foreword is that, like David, I too am smack dab in the middle of writing a comprehensive series on cryptids. While David's series is broken up by State, mine is broken up by time period, covering cryptid sightings and UFOs as seen in the Wild West and Pioneer Period of the United States. But, I'm only on book four of what I hope will be ten volumes on historical cryptid sightings. This, if I'm not mistaken, is David's 8th book overall in a series that will eventually number 50 books—one for each state! Needless to say, this is a daunting task for anyone, but I believe if anyone can, David can. This isn't just because David is a determined researcher, but because he is also well-liked within the cryptid-community. I have yet to come across anyone who doesn't like David, which speaks well of his character, and explains why so many researchers are eager to assist him in his quest to catalogue cryptids state by state.

But then again, all the cryptozoologists I've crossed paths with so far have been very nice, and not territorial at all like the cryptids they chronicle. Perhaps that's because we are all truth seekers here, and uncovering the truth is the top priority rather than bolstering our egos through various discoveries or stories that we wish to proclaim ownership over. David's books have greatly helped me in building my *Cowboys & Saurians* series. His research into the Shunka Warak'in and the Wahoo was invaluable to me in my book *Cowboys & Saurians: Ice Age*. By the same token, I'm pleased that I was able to help him find a very unique Montana Saurian account (though I believe Jerome Clark dug it up long before I did).

Perhaps another reason for the camaraderie amongst the cryptid community is that we've all had to deal with skeptics—and something we all probably share as monster lovers are eye-rolls from friends and acquaintances of the skeptical persuasion. However, many skeptics have never done their own investigations into the unknown. Skeptics like to think that the people telling these tales are either crazy or are just making them up for attention. Many times, the witnesses behind the so-called "kooky" stories are normal people who didn't set out to see anything strange, nor are they seeking an inordinate amount of attention. I once interviewed a night nurse in Roswell, the late Josephine Morones, who saw what appeared to be an alien ghost at the New Mexico Rehabilitation Clinic. Some would dismiss this story on the grounds of the sighting alone, but Josephine was a perfectly normal person. I don't disbelieve a story based on what it entails, but based upon who told it, and I trusted Josephine's testimony. Furthermore, all of the staff at the clinic attested to paranormal activity there. That's a whole building of people that back up each other's claims, but skeptics will reject the "alien ghost" story on the grounds that it is simply too far out for them. Never mind the character of the witness who saw it, or that other witnesses corroborated their claims. Such things simply cannot be, and that is that for many disbelievers.

But, as I write this, times are finally changing. For years, UFOs and aliens were met with the same eye-rolls that Bigfoot was. As of 2021, the government and mainstream media seem to have joined forces in persuading the public to accept the existence of UFOs. Oddly, many of the old-school UFO skeptics weren't so vocal anymore. Suddenly, because the news has said it's OK to believe in such things, people no longer approach the subject of UFOs with such trepidation. But here I am talking about UFOs again when you are here for the cryptids. I suppose my point is, with UFOs finally being acknowledged—some might even say "pushed"—by the mainstream media after years of ridicule, perhaps the existence of cryptids will follow suit? And if that day comes, people like you, me, and David can all sit back and smile. After all, we knew all along.

John LeMay

Introduction

Montana, the Treasure State. Land of shining mountains and vast expanses. According to some, it is the last best place.

The fourth largest state in the union has a lot of nicknames and slogans that describe its landscape, but perhaps the most fitting is "Big Sky Country," a moniker that conveys the sweeping views, rugged terrain, and of course, beautiful western skies.

Montana is located in the northwestern United States with its northern border abutting the southern border of Canada. It also shares borders with the states of Idaho, Wyoming, and North and South Dakota.

The state was admitted to the Union in 1889, becoming the forty-first state of the United States. Despite its late addition as a state, Montana has a rich history. According to the official state website, Montana is home to seven "Indian reservations as well as the state-recognized Little Shell Tribe of Chippewa." The Crow, Northern Cheyenne, Blackfeet, and Chippewa Cree are among the native nations that call Montana home. The largest reservations are the Blackfeet, Crow, Flathead, and Fort Peck reservations.

When early explorers arrived in Montana, it was mainly due to the fur trade. Early explorers were greeted with a land of abundance and even today, the state is rich in wildlife and natural resources.

Montana covers over 147,000 square miles and is home to just over a million people. It is the eight least populous state in the Union. Population density is low, and the state ranks third-least densely populated. In short, Montana has a lot of land and a relatively small number of citizens.

The terrain is widely varied, from mountain ranges

and lush valleys to northern plains, tableland prairies, and badlands, Montana has a lot of natural diversity. There's also an abundance of fresh water in the state with thousands of named rivers and creeks.

Montana's Bitterroot Mountains are one of the longest continuous ranges in the Rocky Mountain chain from Alaska to Mexico, and they divide the state from neighboring Idaho. The southern third of the Bitterroot range blends into the Continental Divide.

For decades, Montana has been cattle country, with ranching and agriculture being the primary sources of income. In recent years, tourism has become a booming industry with current statistics indicating that around thirteen million tourists visit the state annually. Much of the tourism is focused on Montana's outdoor recreation areas. The state has nine National Park Service areas, including the well-known Glacier National Park, Yellowstone National Park, and the Lewis & Clark National Historic Trail. Recreational areas like the Rattlesnake National Recreation Area and Flathead Lake draw outdoor enthusiasts to the state year around for a variety of activities from fishing to boating and skiing, to hiking and camping.

Montana's largest city is Billings, coming in at a little more than 100,000 people. The state capitol is Helena, a city which has just under 30,000 residents. These small population numbers are a further indication that "big city" life is not the thing in Montana. Most of the state consists of small, rural communities and large stretches of ranchland. By all indications, most of the people in the state prefer it that way.

There's an abundance of wildlife in the state of Montana, from large species like the American bison, grizzly bear, caribou, and cougar, to smaller mammals such as beaver, porcupine, and badgers. Aquatic life is abundant, too, and there are almost a hundred species of fish living in the state.

Then there's the other, unofficial wildlife species that purportedly roam the state.

Legends of Bigfoot can be found in the tales and traditions of the state's Native American tribes, and the creatures are still spotted in modern times, from one end of the state to the other. Law enforcement officers even took part in tracking the creatures and their activity in the 1970s.

The beautiful Flathead Lake, a hotspot for water sports and outdoor activity, is said to have its own Loch Ness-style monster dubbed "Flessie" by locals. Is it a giant fish or something else?

And there's more. A band of little people are said to live in the Pryor Mountains, some residents have spotted thunderbirds soaring in the skies, and the state is also home to the mysterious cryptid known as the Shunka Warak'in.

So, settle in and take a trip as we explore the Monsters of Big Sky Country.

MONSTERS OF BIG SKY COUNTRY by David Weatherly

PART ONE
The Shunka Warak'in

The Shunka Warak'in

In 1886, a strange creature was terrorizing settlers in Madison Valley. For a month, the beast preyed on cows and sheep in the region. According to area residents, the creature emitted a disturbing, bloodcurdling cry and many locals were afraid to confront the beast.

Israel Ammon Hutchins was not afraid of the creature. A rugged, Mormon rancher, Hutchins spotted the thing on his property and shot at it. Unfortunately, he missed and killed one of his own cows.

Hutchins got another chance at the animal when it made a return visit to his ranch. The second time was the charm for Hutchins, and he shot and killed the beast. Purportedly, as the creature lay dying, it used the last of its energy to try to reach, and harm, Hutchins and his family.

Israel Hutchins's son remembered the creature's haunting screams echoing at night and said that when it was in its death throes, the creature bit through a half inch rope with a single bite. According to Hutchins, the creature "exerted his very last strength to reach any one of us."

Hoping to recoup the loss of his cow, the rancher traded the body of the unusual creature to a local taxidermist, Joseph Sherwood. Sherwood stuffed the animal and put it on display in his shop, a combination general store and museum, across the state border in Henry's Lake, Idaho.

But what was the creature? No one seemed to be sure, but there were plenty of speculations. Some compared it to an African hyena, and inevitably, stories of escaped circus animals were thrown into the speculative mix to explain the creature.

Others thought it was something even more exotic, perhaps

a species that had never been seen before, while other people simply thought it was a wolf.

While at first glance the creature seems to be a one-of-a-kind beast, there may be more of a history of such things in the region than many realize.

In my book, *Silver State Monsters: Cryptids & Legends of Nevada*, I covered the tale of the "wahoo," a creature that surfaced in northern Nevada in the late 1800s. Accounts of the wahoo bear a striking similarity to reports of the Shunka Warak'in in Montana.

According to the first purported sighting of the wahoo, it was a four-legged beast with a long, slender body and a medium length tail that curved up and over its back. The animal's legs were short, and it had large paws and long claws. It was covered with long, fine hair that was mostly black with some white spots.

The wahoos were said to be larger than a coyote with an average weight of between fifty and seventy-five pounds.

As the tales multiplied, descriptions of the beast began to vary. A report in the *Reno Gazette* in 1880 described the creature this way:

"Five foot three inches from one track to the other, its tail about the length of its body, with a bunch of red hair on the tip; a stripe down the back about four inches; deep red stripes running with the ribs; his ears shaped like a hog's standing straight out; two tusks two inches long on each side of his mouth above and below."

Reports of the wahoo soon spread and there were claims that the beast, or one like it, was wandering around in Idaho and Montana.

It's easy to assume that all the published accounts of wahoos were complete fabrication, but other factors come into play when examining the history of the strange creature. Obviously, people of the time believed the accounts. It was, after all, the wild west and there was much still undiscovered.

Intrigued by accounts of the weird creatures, some hunters

set off on the trail, hoping to bag a specimen of the beast. Some came back with accounts of the wahoo living in the wild. The beast, they reported, was vicious and frightening.

One pair of hunters reported a wahoo that growled viciously at them when they approached it. One of the men impaled the creature with a hayfork when it leapt at him. The other man had his foot mutilated when the animal attacked him. Both men reported that the animal had a "very offensive scent." Neither of the hunters took the creature's hide and it is unknown what became of the bodies.

Was it a wahoo that Hutchins's brought down? Whether he or any of his neighbors had heard of the wahoo is unknown and without multiple bodies to compare, it's difficult to say, but at the least, the similarity in tales is of interest.

As for Sherwood, once he had possession of the creature and stuffed it, he dubbed the specimen a "ringdocus."

The unusual taxidermy of the animal remained on display at Sherwood's iconic location for many years, then sometime in the 1980's it mysteriously disappeared.

The story of the odd creature had largely been forgotten and it became a footnote in local folklore until 1977. At that time, Hutchins' grandson, naturalist Ross Hutchins, mentioned the story in his book, *Trails to Nature's Mysteries: The Life of a Working Naturalist*.

Hutchins's book recounted the story of the beast and included an old photo of the stuffed and mounted creature that had plagued his grandfather and other Montana settlers.

The Madison River Valley

What's in a Name?

Cryptozoologists had certainly been aware of the story of the beast. Loren Coleman and Jerome Clark's *Cryptozoology A to Z* contained an entry on the ringdocus in conjunction with the Native American legend of an animal called the "Shunka Warak'in." The animal is reputed to resemble a wolf, hyena, or even a hybrid of the two. Coleman says the name itself is derived from a native word meaning "carries off dogs," or, "carrying-off dogs." A Native American resident of Montana contacted Coleman regarding the creatures. As detailed in Coleman and Clark's *Cryptozoology A to Z*:

"In 1995, Lance Foster, an Ioway Indian, told Loren Coleman: 'We had a strange animal called Shunka Warak'in that snuck into camps at night and stole dogs. It was said to look something like a hyena and cried like a person when they killed it. Its skin is said to be kept by someone still.'"

Foster, who had heard of the mounted ringdocus, thought it was an example of the Shunka Warak'in.

Coleman has also noted that the description of the Shunka Warak'in is similar to that of borophagus, a hyena-like dog that lived in North America from the Middle Miocene epoch through the Late Pliocene epoch.

Borophagus was believed to be about the size of a modern coyote with a bulging forehead and powerful set of "bone crunching" jaws. The species was very successful in North America and at one time there were over a dozen species of them.

Lance Foster found another Native American connection to the creature while he was attending Iowa State University in 1991. Foster was working on a degree in Anthropology and his thesis subject was the sacred bundle system of his tribe, the Ioway. During his research, Foster delved into the notes of Alanson Skinner who had collected Ioway tribal artifacts in the 1900s. One item listed in Skinner's notes caught Foster's attention. It was listed as a "Big Ioway War Bundle" and reportedly contained a "hyena skin."

On his Paranormal Montana blog, Foster shared this passage from Skinner's fieldnotes:

"Once a long time [ago], every night some dogs were gone, and the people in the village and the young men got up a war party. They thought it was [the] enemy [who was stealing the dogs] and laid for it. They had the horses and so on, and when this thing came, they fought it like a person and killed it. When it died, it cried like a person. That is why they put it in the bundle, because it seemed to have a power. They shot at him a lot of times and never killed him and followed him a day and a half. They painted the hide and used it in war to keep from being hit. [The hide was] worn across the shoulder."

The passage may sound somewhat contradictory since the storyteller first mentions the death of the creature and then says it was shot many times but not killed. But I believe this is merely the writer's difficulty in relating the information given by the native elder.

Foster also clarifies the proper spelling and pronunciation of the word:

"In simpler modern Ioway transcription, 'Carries-off-dogs' would be normally written as shunka warak'in (SHOON-kah wah-rahk-EEn) (the final 'n' is not pronounced, but just nasalizes the EE sound before it). Shunka = dog. Wa= something, ra=mouth, k'in= to carry (Good Tracks, Iowa-Otoe-Missouria Language 1992: 117, etc.). Literally, 'something that carries dogs in its mouth.'"

Skinner himself mentions the topic in his *Ethnology of the Ioway Indians* and adds that the information came from Chief David Tohee and Joseph Springer. The version found in the book is slightly longer than that found in Skinner's field notes and is worth noting here:

"One time the people began to miss their dogs. Every morning a few were gone, and no one knew the cause. Some thought it the work of an enemy, so the young men got up a war party and hid themselves so as to surprise and kill the nightly visitor. It turned out to be a strange animal, different from anything they had ever seen before. They named it 'Carrying-off-dogs,' but it is very like the animal the white people keep in their shows today and call hyena. When it entered the camp, the young warriors attacked it just as if it was a person. Again, and again, they shot at this creature, and could not kill it, but after following it a day and a half they at last succeeded in putting it to death. When it died, it cried just like a human being. When they heard this and thought of the hard time they had in killing it, they decided that it must be a creature of great power. So, they skinned it, and painted its hide, and later placed the hide in with the other powerful objects in the war bundle, to wear in battle across the shoulder to turn away flying bullets and arrows. But before the hide was put in the bundle, a big dance was held. Immediately afterward a party set out and were very successful, as they killed a number of enemies, returning with many scalps."

Foster notes that it would be interesting to track down the Ioway bundle that contained the animal skin, but he confirms that the collections were split up with portions now in museum collections in both Washington, D.C. and New York.

So, Shunka Warak'in or ringdocous? To further confuse the matter, another name was also thrown around to identify the creature—the "guyasticutus."

Purportedly, the guyasticutus is the scientific name for the "rocky mountain hyena," but far from being a scientific name, the word doesn't mean anything. As John Kern and Irwin Griggs say in *This America*:

"Still other words got into the American language from nowhere; like Topsy, they just grew. Witness guyasticutus:

"The guyasticutus was—or still is, for all we know—the most ferocious, rambunctious, man-eating wild animal ever exhibited under canvas to gullible Americans. For only ten

17

cents, ladeez and gentlemen, a tenth part of a dollar, you can come into the tent and see with your own eyes this horrendous beast which consumes forty-eleven men, women, and tender babes-in-arms at a gulp, then bellows for forty-eleven more.

"No one except its proprietor, alas, has ever actually seen the guyasticutus for just when the crowd around the entrances has bought the last ticket, the proprietor rushes out of the tent and roars, 'Run for your lives, ladeez and gentlemen! Escape before you are swallowed alive! The guyasticutus has busted loose!'"

Some think that the name guyasticutus was a product of traveling sideshows hoping to lure in gullible patrons and sell tickets for a chance to see the beast, but photos of the taxidermy mount have included the name as a label for the beast.

Interestingly, a woman named Barbie Kirby Austin commented on one of Lance Foster's online articles about the Shunka Warak'in and offered some interesting input.

As it turns out, Austin is the great granddaughter of I.A. Hutchins and the daughter of Jack Kirby, the man who rediscovered the taxidermy of the creature. She writes: "The Guyasticutus is what we grew up calling him."

Another post on the same thread, this one anonymous, is reportedly from Joseph Sherwood's great grandson. He reports a similar memory:

"I spent many years visiting my grandparents while residing in West Yellowstone, MT. And many years visiting my Aunt Dewey as she maintained the museum until her passing.

"We all knew the animal as the Guyasticutus as well, not the other names attached to it today."

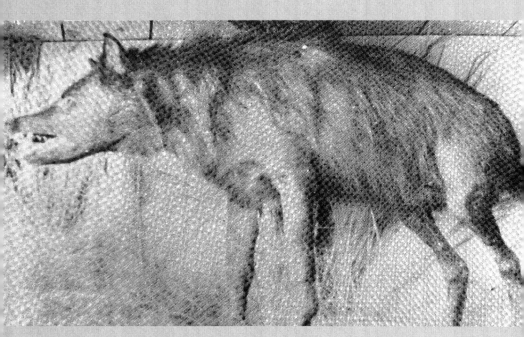

The taxidermy of the beast killed by Hutchins.
Photo by Ross Hutchins.

The Taxidermy Trail

Photos are one thing, but what about the actual specimen of the creature? By all accounts, it was still around to be seen in the Sherwood Museum until the location closed in the late 1970s. The family finally sold the museum and the surrounding property in the 1990s to Steve and Carol Burk of Idaho Falls, Idaho.

Prior to the sale of the property, the Sherwood family donated the museum's artifacts, including the taxidermy mounts, to the Idaho State Historical Society. It was later learned that the items had been placed in storage, and there, they stayed tucked away until the early 2000s when Jack Kirby, a descendent of Israel Ammon Hutchins, sought out the artifact and located it in museum storage.

The November 14, 2007, edition of the *Bozeman Daily Chronicle* announced: "Mystery monster returns home after 121 years." The paper reported:

"The only evidence of the creature's existence was a missing taxidermy mount and a grainy black-and-white photograph of that mount—which fueled strange speculation about what kind of animal it really was.

"Now after 121 years, the taxidermy mount has been found. The creature that once spooked some of the Madison Valley's first white settlers has come home."

Ross Hutchins's written account stated that the animal was almost completely black, and he said the back sloped downward like a hyena. With the creature relocated, new details emerged.

The specimen of the animal measures 48 inches from the tip of its snout to its rump, not including the tail, and stands 28 inches high at the shoulder. It has a sloping back and a strangely shaped head with a narrow snout. The coat is dark brown, almost black, with lighter tan colored areas and the faint impression of stripes on its side.

Surprisingly, the taxidermy was found to be in good condition despite its age and its time in storage.

One would expect, or at least hope, that the rediscovery of the specimen would help bring some answers to the mystery of the beast's identity, but sadly, this has not been the case.

Initially, it was hoped that with the specimen available, DNA testing could be done to determine more about the creature; however, arguments soon arose over ownership of the piece.

Reportedly, when the state took possession of the items from the Sherwood collection, officials said they would hold the items until they could be properly displayed in Island Park.

The Island Park Historical Society (IPHS) helped arrange the agreement between the Sherwood family and the state and for years, the IPHS tried to raise money to build a museum for local history.

When Kirby arranged to have the specimen put on display in Montana, members of the IPHS board of directors as well as local residents were concerned that it would not be returned to Idaho.

The *Island Park News* had published stories on the creature, generally referring to it as the "Sherwood Beast," a semihumorous Halloween tale written by Elizabeth Laden for several years running.

Reflecting the aggravation that many were expressing on the topic, Elizabeth Laden wrote an article in the paper's December 7, 2007, edition that proclaimed: "The Sherwood Beast of Island Park legend and lore has been kidnapped!"

Laden referred to Walt Williams's article for the *Bozeman Chronicle* that announced the monster's "return home after 121 years."

The point of offense, Laden said, was the implication that the specimen "belonged" to Montana rather than Idaho where it had been since it had first been mounted.

Nothing, it seems, has been simple about the beast, its identity, or even its death.

When Jack Kirby took the specimen to Montana, he carried it to the gravesite of his ancestor Israel Hutchins who had shot it.

According to the story, Hutchins had killed the creature in 1886 on what is now the Sun Ranch property, but even that is disputed.

The article in *Island Park News* reported that Hutchins was not the monster's killer, as Laden writes:

"Mack's Inn resident Harold Bishop did some research on the beast for a scout project. He interviewed a Chester resident, Pete Marx, who told him a range rider named Heini Schooster killed the beast that was displayed in the museum. Schooster lived down the Madison River from the old Cliff Lake Post Office, which is not that far from the Sun Ranch.

"Bishop's story had Schooster killing the beast with a lever action .32 special. Kirby claims the fatal shot was fired with a G.W. Morse rifle—caliber is not given."

Israel Hutchins's great granddaughter, Barbie Kirby Austin, has something to say on the matter, too:

"Heini Schooster did not kill this animal. His place was six miles from where I.A. Hutchins lived with his family. The animal was killed right outside their front door.

"Heini lived down near the West Fork where the Kirby Ranch is; however, the animal was killed on the Sun Ranch." (from comments on Lance Foster's Paranormal Montana blog)

Austin goes on to argue why the creature should remain in Montana.

Cryptozoologists, and other interested parties, pushed for a DNA test of the creature, but even that was a contentious topic. Since the specimen was owned by one institution but being displayed by another it was unclear who had the rights in determining when or if a DNA test could be done.

As if such levels of confusion and debate were not enough, some people have suggested that the specimen on display is not even the original monster that was killed and put on display in the Sherwood museum, claiming there are differences between the specimen and the photos of the original beast that Hutchins killed.

Proponents of this theory suggest that a modern fake was constructed to resemble the famous creature.

To date, there is no further clarity on the identity of the beast. Some still argue that it is simply a wolf, while others point to more exotic origins. Whatever the case, it remains on display at the Madison Valley History Association's Museum in Ennis, Montana.

The Creature of McCone County

In December 2005, a strange creature started attacking and killing livestock in Montana. The beast was spotted in several areas, including McCone, Garfield, and Dawson counties.

The death toll from the creature climbed quickly. By March 2006, it had struck six herds of sheep in McCone and Garfield counties, wounding 71 and killing 36 ewes.

The thing had even earned its own local nickname, "The Creature of McCone County." Despite the local moniker, the story went national in May 2006 when an article appeared in USA Today.

The beast continued to attack livestock and by October 2006, it had racked up about 120 victims.

Ranchers were angry and wanted action. Their animals and their livelihood were being attacked by an elusive creature and something had to be done. Even more disturbing for some was the news that the creature was not alone.

Writing in *New West* for the March 29, 2006, issue, reporter Hal Herring writes:

"The creature, whatever it is, came out of Montana's own McCone County, wandering from the rough breaks of Timber Creek, just south of the Big Dry Arm of Fort Peck Reservoir and the CM Russell Wildlife Refuge. Where it had wandered before that, Canada or North Dakota, nobody knows."

"The creature is a traveler, and it is not always alone, though its companion leaves a smaller track still, adding to the mystery."

Herring also noted how disturbing many of the kill sites were:

"John McKerlick found, according to an account in the Jordan Tribune, '...lambs with meat, hide and wool dragging on the ground; their insides torn out and a front leg on one torn away. Ten were dead and eight still going...He found two more dead and a 100–110-pound lamb had been eaten and dragged in a 20' diameter circle.' Whatever killed the sheep had stayed in the area for a long time, leaving a lot of tracks. 'We had an overflow from a watertank that was frozen and held the snow, and he sauntered around all over that ice," McKerlick said. "I don't know what he was doing all that time.'"

Many people in the area were convinced the culprit, or culprits, were wolves, and angry ranchers wanted wildlife officials to do something—or else they would take matters into their own hands. The difficulty, for ranchers at least, is that wolves are on the endangered list and cannot be killed.

The topic of wolves has long been a flashpoint for argument in Montana. The animals were hunted almost to extinction until they were designated an endangered species in 1973. Since that time, there have been frequent arguments between ranchers and wildlife groups who wanted the animals reintroduced into the wild. In the mid-1990s, 31 wolves from Canada were transferred into central Idaho and Yellowstone National Park.

The distance did little to satisfy ranchers who opposed the plan. Even officials were aware that the distance didn't necessarily mean the wolves wouldn't make it to ranch lands. Carolyn Sime, a wolf coordinator for the state's Fish, Wildlife and Parks Department, points out that "Wolves are fabulous travelers. In 2004, a radio-collared wolf from Yellowstone was struck and killed about 420 miles away, on Interstate 70 west of Denver."

After rounds of discussions, and a fight against bureaucratic red tape, ranchers finally got their wish and USDA officials issued a kill order for a pair of wolves believed to be responsible for livestock deaths in the area.

During a flyover of the area by officials from the state's Fish, Wildlife and Parks Department, a pair of wolves were spotted. One was described as a young female, charcoal gray in color;

the second was not described. Wolf coordinator Carolyn Sime speculated that the wolves could be from the Northern Rockies, but also noted they might be domestic bred wolves or wolf hybrids that had been the product of manipulated breeding.

On December 9, 2006, the *Billings Gazette* reported that the mystery animal, the one that may have been attacking sheep, was killed from the air by Montana's Wildlife Services agents on November 2, 2006. According to the article in the *Gazette*:

"What they shot, it is believed, is the 'Creature.' But now they aren't exactly sure what it is they killed. The animal was big at 106 pounds. Its color seems unexpected for a wolf. The animal shot in Garfield County had shades of orange, red and yellow in its fur, unlike the Northern Rockies wolves, which tend more toward grays, browns, and black, said wildlife officials."

The animal's carcass was sent to the National Fish and Wildlife Forensics Laboratory in Ashland, Oregon, for genetic study, and a sample for DNA analysis was sent to experts at the University of California in Los Angeles.

Speculations continued to run wild after the creature was shot. Some speculated that it was a wolf hybrid that had been genetically altered, hence, its unusual appearance.

It took officials some time to report their conclusions, but the final conclusion was that the creature was a domestic wolf that had either escaped from captivity or had been turned loose into the wild.

Officially, the killing of wolves is strictly regulated in the state of Montana, although there are some notable exceptions. If a wolf gets too close and is threatening people or livestock it can be shot.

On May 16, 2018, a rancher near the town of Denton said a wolf-like creature was indeed too close and he shot and killed it.

State wildlife officials were initially unable to determine what species the animal was. While it looked like a wolf, its teeth were too short, its front paws were abnormally small, and its claws too large.

The *Great Falls Tribune* gave the creature-shooting a front-page spot and noted the unusual characteristics:

"Was it a wolf, some type of hybrid, or a creature that hasn't been seen in Montana since the Ice Age?"

Bruce Auchly, spokesman for the FWP, told the paper, "We have no idea what this was until we get a DNA report back. It was near a rancher's place, it was shot, and our game wardens went to investigate. The whole animal was sent to our lab in Bozeman."

Photos of the creature showed an unusual looking animal, raggedy in appearance with what appeared to be short legs and a large head and snout. The animal measured 45 inches from the tip of the nose to the rump and weighed 84.5 pounds.

Once photos of the unusual creature hit social media, there was a frenzy of speculation as people tried to guess the creature's identity. Some were positive it was a known animal with guesses ranging from a hybrid dog to grizzly bear. Other theories suggested the beast was something prehistoric, perhaps a dire wolf or other ancient creature. Others went further, speculating that the creature was a werewolf or dogman.

The *Tribune* published one unidentified commentator's suggestion that the creature was a dogman:

"That could very well be what's being called Dogman. They're spotted each day and the government quells any and all reports. Several people report being strong armed into keeping quiet about their reports by men wearing black suits. These are just facts. Look into it if you don't believe me."

The wide range of theories aside, officials were admittedly baffled by the creature's appearance. Ty Smucker, a wolf management specialist for the Montana FWP, told the paper that several things grabbed his attention about the beast:

"The ears are too big. The legs look a little short. The feet look a little small, and the coat looks weird. There's just something off about it."

On June 19, the *Tribune* reported that the DNA test had come back on the creature—according to Mary Curtis, a geneticist at the Oregon lab, "In this case, there was very, very little if any support for the animal being a dog, coyote, or hybrid. It was very strongly placed in the wolf category."

According to the paper, a full inspection of the animal at the wildlife lab in Bozeman revealed that it was a dark brown wolf. Curtis noted that the wolf was young and still small and that the unusual aspects of the creature were simply due to variability in the species.

While the case is officially closed, and despite the official report, some still believe that something more unusual than a normal wolf was shot in the spring of 2018.

One person I spoke with in Kalispel told me he didn't believe the official report, positing that the government was covering up something that would panic people if it got out. He said, "There's a lot of strange things in Montana, and there are a lot of people who keep those things secret."

For the curious minded, the question remains, what prowls in the back country of the Treasure State? Shunka Warak'in, ringdocus, guyasticutus, Rocky Mountain hyena, or just plain wolf?

Until the next strange creature steps out of the shadows, we can only wait and ponder the possibilities.

MONSTERS OF BIG SKY COUNTRY by David Weatherly

PART TWO
Sasquatch in the Treasure State

Big Sky Country

Native Tales and Early Accounts

Sasquatch researchers believe the state of Montana has all the key elements needed to make it a likely location for Bigfoot to hide out. A quick survey of the state and its resources makes it easy to see why this would be the case. The abundance of food and fresh water, along with the vast portions of uninhabited or sparsely populated land, would provide everything an elusive creature like Bigfoot would want.

Despite the low population numbers, encounters certainly do occur. Through the years, ranchers, tourists, and everyday residents, have had brushes with hairy bipedal creatures on the state's highways and in remote areas of the back country.

Encounters in the state are not new, however, and there's a solid history of sightings from around Montana.

Native traditions from the region contain many tales of the creatures and even today, the creature shows up on Native land on occasion.

Many early explorers of the region heard Native American tales of aggressive giants that threatened tribal members and remained a danger in the vast wilderness territories of the state.

When Lewis and Clark trekked across to the Pacific Northwest, they encountered numerous tribes along the way and listened to many traditional tales, hoping to learn more about the land. During their time in what is now Montana, members of the expedition met a group of Flathead natives in the western Bitterroot Valley. It was the first time the Flatheads had seen whites, and the meeting was a peaceful one. The Flatheads shared food with the white explorers and recounted some of their tribal lore to the party, including tales of creatures they called "Natliskeliguten." Roughly translated the term

*Lewis & Clark heard tales of strange creatures
during their journey west.*

means "killers of men."

According to the Flatheads, the Natliskeliguten were powerful giants that had once roamed the area in large numbers. Reportedly, by the time of the Lewis and Clark expedition, the giants' numbers had been reduced, but they were still present and considered very dangerous. One traditional Flathead story gives a glimpse of the giants' power:

"Once when a small hunting party came upon a giant asleep in the forest, they tied him with ropes of buffalo hair, sat upon his chest, and beat him until he wakened. Then he laughed thunderously, burst the ropes, and sent the men flying through the air as he rose to his feet. Seizing one of them by the ankle, he tossed the man across the Missoula River."

According to the Flatheads, the giants were physical creatures, not a part of the spirit world. Much like modern Sasquatch encounters, the giants made great effort to avoid being seen by humans, but the tales were abundant among the people. According to historian H.H. Turney-High:

"Fully half of the Flathead stories deal with these giants, and easily two-thirds of them mention them."

The Kootenai tribe of Idaho and northern Montana have similar tales of giants in the region. According to tribal member William Gingrass, the giants were greatly feared by the people because they preyed on humans. Gingrass said it was known that the giants followed the waterways and if someone ventured to the water's edge the giants would kill and eat them. According to Gingrass:

"My great-grandmother's uncle once found the skeleton of a giant, buried in a sitting position, in a grave near Superior." (a town in Mineral County, MT).

The Coeur d' A'lene nation, who lived west of the Flatheads and Kootenai in what is now Idaho, also have tales of giants. According to the Coeur d' A'lene, the monsters were as tall as a tipi, had a strong odor "like that of a burning horn," and had black faces. According to tribal lore, the giants lived in nearby caves and often stole fish out of the people's traps.

On the eastern side of Montana, the Sioux nation have tales of hairy giants, too. Reno First, a full-blooded Yankton Sioux and Montana native, spoke with the *Great Falls Tribune* in 1977 and recounted a traditional Sioux tale of the creatures. According to First, stories of the creature go far back in Sioux traditional lore.

"Our tribe traveled in what would now be the area from the Black Hills through western South Dakota, North Dakota, and into Montana and Saskatchewan."

First recounts the story of a group of hunters who found a place with "many caves." Two of the men, a youth in his early 20s and an older man, decided to venture into the caves to see what was inside. The men found themselves in a cave with crystalized rock that glowed in spots, allowing them to see inside the cave. As First recounts:

"After some time, they came to a place where the glow seemed stronger, creating a lighted hallway. They noticed the passageway turned at an angle in the light.

"A strong odor came to their nostrils. Rounding the bend, they came upon a large, hairy creature sleeping against one wall. As they stopped and stared at the strange sight, the creature raised its head, blinked open its eyes and stared back. The men turned and ran."

The men raced to get out of the cave, climbing back up and falling outside of the entrance, to the astonishment of their companions who had been waiting to see what they had discovered in the cave. The two men were in a state of shock.

"Their knees, elbows and shoulders were cut and bleeding from falling down and bumping into the walls of the cave. Both were covered with sweat; foam was coming out of their mouths."

The men were taken back to camp and tended to. By the next day, they had recovered enough to tell their tale. Some of the tribe believed them, others did not, but further proof soon came.

A few days later, the older man who had dared the cave was

hunting with another companion. As the two were observing some deer, they had a strange sighting:

"Moving slowly though the brush was a big hairy creature similar to the one in the cave. Its body hair was reddish in color, and it seemed to be stalking deer. Ducking out of sight, the men quickly gathered their horses and raced back to camp with the news. The tribe immediately broke camp and moved north."

Whether or not the Sioux found a place free of the hairy giants isn't quite clear. At the least, tribal members do still report encounters on their current reservation lands. It's important to note that the tribe's traditions say the creature is ancient. Some refer to the hairy biped as "Chiye-tanka," or Big Man. Peter Matthiessen even mentions the Big Man in his bestseller *In the Spirit of Crazy Horse*. According to the book:

"They exist in another dimension from us but can appear in this dimension whenever they have a reason to. See, it's like there are many levels, many dimensions. When our time in this one is finished, we move on to the next, but the Big Man can go between. The Big Man comes from God. He's our big brother, kind of looks out for us."

Perhaps the most significant historical account related to Bigfoot in Montana comes from none other than the 26th president of the United States, Theodore Roosevelt.

Not only was Roosevelt a noted statesman and politician, but he was also a naturalist, writer, and conservationist. As an avid hunter, he spent a lot of time in the wild and later wrote about his adventures. Roosevelt was a practical man and was not one to back down from challenges or buy into outrageous tales; much of this attitude came from his time on the frontier. As he wrote:

"Frontiersmen are not, as a rule, apt to be very superstitious. They lead lives too hard and practical and have too little imagination in things spiritual and supernatural. I have heard but few ghost stories while living on the frontier, and these few were of a perfectly commonplace and conventional type."

President Theodore Roosevelt.

One of the tales Roosevelt heard on the frontier involved a man named Bauman and a deadly encounter in the wilds of Montana. Roosevelt told the story in his book, *The Wilderness Hunter*, first published in 1893. The account is lengthy but given its historical importance I present it here in its entirety to convey both the details and flavor of the original account:

"I once listened to a goblin story which rather impressed me. It was told by a grizzled, weather-beaten old mountain hunter, named Bauman, who was born and had passed all his life on the frontier. He must have believed what he said, for he could hardly repress a shudder at certain points of the tale; but he was of German ancestry, and in childhood had doubtless been saturated with all kinds of ghost and goblin lore, so that many fearsome superstitions were latent in his mind; besides, he knew well the stories told by the Indian medicine men in their winter camps, of the snow-walkers, and the specters, and the formless evil beings that haunt the forest depths, and dog and waylay the lonely wanderer who after nightfall passes through the regions where they lurk; and it may be that when overcome by the horror of the fate that befell his friend, and when oppressed by the awful dread of the unknown, he grew to attribute, both at the time and still more in remembrance, weird and elfin traits to what was merely some abnormally wicked and cunning beast; but whether this was so or not, no man can say.

"When the event occurred, Bauman was still a young man, and was trapping with a partner among the mountains dividing the forks of Salmon from the head of Wisdom River. Not having had much luck, he and his partner determined to go up into a particularly wild and lonely pass through which ran a small stream said to contain many beaver. The pass had an evil reputation because the year before a solitary hunter who had wandered into it was there slain, seemingly by a wild beast, the half-eaten remains being afterwards found by some mining prospectors who had passed his camp only the night before.

"The memory of this event, however, weighed very lightly with the two trappers, who were as adventurous and hardy as others of their kind. They took their two lean mountain ponies to the foot of the pass where they left them in an open beaver meadow, the rocky timber-clad ground being from there onward impracticable for horses. They then struck out on foot through the vast, gloomy forest, and in about four hours reached a little open glade where they concluded to camp, as signs of game were plenty.

"There was still an hour of daylight left, and after building a brush lean-to and throwing down and opening their packs, they started upstream. The country was very dense and hard to travel through, as there was much down timber, although here and there the somber woodland was broken by small glades of mountain grass. At dusk they again reached camp. The glade in which it was pitched was not many yards wide, the tall, close-set pines and firs rising round it like a wall. On one side was a little stream, beyond which rose the steep mountain slope, covered with the unbroken growth of evergreen forest.

"They were surprised to find that during their absence something, apparently a bear, had visited camp, and had rummaged about among their things, scattering the contents of their packs, and in sheer wantonness destroying their lean-to. The footprints of the beast were quite plain, but at first, they paid no particular heed to them, busying themselves with rebuilding the lean-to, laying out their beds and stores and lighting the fire.

"While Bauman was making ready supper, it being already dark, his companion began to examine the tracks more closely, and soon took a brand from the fire to follow them up, where the intruder had walked along a game trail after leaving the camp. When the brand flickered out, he returned and took another, repeating his inspection of the footprints very closely.

"Coming back to the fire, he stood by it a minute or two, peering out into the darkness, and suddenly remarked, 'Bauman, that bear has been walking on two legs.'

"Bauman laughed at this, but his partner insisted that he was right, and upon again examining the tracks with a torch, they certainly did seem to be made by but two paws or feet. However, it was too dark to make sure. After discussing whether the footprints could possibly be those of a human being and coming to the conclusion that they could not be, the two men rolled up in their blankets, and went to sleep under the lean-to. At midnight Bauman was awakened by some noise and sat up in his blankets. As he did so his nostrils were struck by a strong, wild-beast odor, and he caught the loom of a great body in the darkness at the mouth of the lean-to. Grasping his rifle, he fired at the vague, threatening shadow, but must have missed, for immediately afterwards he heard the smashing of the underwood as the thing, whatever it was, rushed off into the impenetrable blackness of the forest and the night.

"After this the two men slept but little, sitting up by the rekindled fire, but they heard nothing more. In the morning they started out to look at the few traps they had set the previous evening and put out new ones. By an unspoken agreement they kept together all day and returned to camp towards evening. On nearing it they saw, hardly to their astonishment, that the lean-to had again been torn down. The visitor of the preceding day had returned, and in wanton malice had tossed about their camp kit and bedding and destroyed the shanty. The ground was marked up by its tracks, and on leaving the camp it had gone along the soft earth by the brook. The footprints were as plain as if on snow, and, after a careful scrutiny of the trail, it certainly did seem as if, whatever the thing was, it had walked off on but two legs.

"The men, thoroughly uneasy, gathered a great heap of dead logs and kept up a roaring fire throughout the night, one or the other sitting on guard most of the time.

"About midnight the thing came down through the forest opposite, across the brook, and stayed there on the hillside for nearly an hour. They could hear the branches crackle as it moved about, and several times it uttered a harsh, grating, long-drawn moan, a peculiarly sinister sound. Yet it did not venture near the fire. In the morning the two trappers, after discussing the strange events of the last 36 hours, decided that they would shoulder their packs and leave the valley that afternoon.

"They were the more ready to do this because in spite of seeing a good deal of game sign they had caught very little fur. However, it was necessary first to go along the line of their traps and gather them, and this they started out to do. All the morning they kept together, picking up trap after trap, each one empty.

"On first leaving camp they had the disagreeable sensation of being followed. In the dense spruce thickets, they occasionally heard a branch snap after they had passed; and now and then there were slight rustling noises among the small pines to one side of them.

"At noon they were back within a couple of miles of camp. In the high, bright sunlight their fears seemed absurd to the two-armed men, accustomed as they were, through long years of lonely wandering in the wilderness, to face every kind of danger from man, brute or element. There were still three beaver traps to collect from a little pond in a wide ravine nearby. Bauman volunteered to gather these and bring them in, while his companion went ahead to camp and made ready the packs.

"On reaching the pond Bauman found three beavers in the traps, one of which had been pulled loose and carried into a beaver house. He took several hours in securing and preparing the beaver, and when he started homewards, he marked, with some uneasiness, how low the sun was getting. As he hurried toward camp, under the tall trees, the silence and desolation of the forest weighed on him. His feet made no sound on the pine needles and the slanting sunrays, striking through among the straight trunks, made a gray twilight in which objects at a distance glimmered indistinctly.

"There was nothing to break the gloomy stillness which, when there is no breeze, always broods over these somber primeval forests. At last, he came to the edge of the little glade where the camp lay and shouted as he approached it but got no answer. The campfire had gone out, though the thin blue smoke was still curling upwards.

"Near it lay the packs wrapped and arranged. At first Bauman could see nobody; nor did he receive an answer to his call. Stepping forward he again shouted, and as he did so his eye fell on the body of his friend, stretched beside the trunk of a great fallen spruce. Rushing towards it the horrified trapper found that the body was still warm, but that the neck was broken, while there were four great fang marks in the throat.

"The footprints of the unknown beast-creature, printed

deep in the soft soil, told the whole story. The unfortunate man, having finished his packing, had sat down on the spruce log with his face to the fire, and his back to the dense woods, to wait for his companion. While thus waiting, his monstrous assailant, which must have been lurking in the woods, waiting for a chance to catch one of the adventurers unprepared, came silently up from behind, walking with long noiseless steps and seemingly still on two legs. Evidently unheard, it reached the man, and broke his neck by wrenching his head back with its fore paws, while it buried its teeth in his throat. It had not eaten the body, but apparently had romped and gamboled around it in uncouth, ferocious glee, occasionally rolling over and over it; and had then fled back into the soundless depths of the woods.

"Bauman, utterly unnerved, and believing that the creature with which he had to deal was something either half human or half devil, some great goblin-beast, abandoned everything but his rifle and struck off at speed down the pass, not halting until he reached the beaver meadows where the hobbled ponies were still grazing. Mounting, he rode onwards through the night, until beyond reach of pursuit."

Is Bauman's tale true? As Roosevelt stated, no man can say. It is at the least a fascinating historical account that fits many of the parameters of stories involving Sasquatch-like creatures.

Typically, newspapers from the 1800s yield a good number of "wild man" reports, but these are scant from the state of Montana.

One story was run in the August 20, 1892, edition of Anaconda's *Standard*. The paper reported that a wild man of sorts was running around in the mountains somewhere near the state's border with Wyoming. As the news reported:

"Some of the old-time hunters and Indian fighters, who are still holding out in the city, should endeavor to find a wild-eyed individual who came in from the mountains this morning. Whether he discovered a new brand of whisky or whether it was the loneliness of this life in the mountains that caused him to see visions and hear sounds is not known, but, whatever the cause, he had told a story that knocks Joe Klaffki's ghost story, attested to by Jack Brennan, completely in the shade. He said that over in the range of mountains which form part of the Wyoming line he had seen evidence of the existence of a creature whose genus was unknown to him. He also claimed to have obtained a glimpse of the "varmit," but always when he was unarmed, and as its appearance was such as not to invite a close inspection, he had never sought to get near enough to see just what it was. He says the animal is covered with hair, but in form it is not unlike a man, a resemblance that is increased by the creature's habit of rising on its haunches and walking on its hind legs after the manner of a gorilla. After having seen the animal, the man said he could account for the existence of the torn and partly eaten carcasses of several large bears and also of one mountain sheep that he claimed to have found in the vicinity of where the unknown animal apparently makes his headquarters. The stranger says he will return to the mountain shortly and will pilot anybody who may desire to visit the locality to the exact spot where he last saw the monster."

Skipping well ahead in time, numerous sources list a weird 1952 sighting, though I have been unable to determine the original source of the report, though it may have come from researcher John Green.

Reportedly, in October 1952, Lyle Slade was hunting elk at Seeley Lake in Missoula County. The hunter spotted what looked like a wounded elk on the opposite side of the clearing he was in. He also heard a strange sound described as a "jabbering noise." As Slade watched, a seven-foot-tall creature crossed the clearing and headed for the wounded elk. The thing was covered with cinnamon colored hair. As if the sight wasn't unusual enough, Slade reported that the creature was wearing a leather belt with a brass buckle.

Ray Crowe also mentions a Seeley Lake incident in *Bigfoot Behavior Volume II*; though no date is given for the report, it involves a freezer-raiding Sasquatch. The incident comes from a woman named Ann who said her grandmother had seen the creature at her home near the lake. The woman reports:

"She heard a noise on the back porch and went to investigate. There was a 'bear' near the freezer by the open door, his head still buried in the freezer. She shouted and the bear stood up and turned to look at her. It nearly gave her a heart attack as the large ape faced her and then quickly walked off the porch into the night."

Crowe also mentions another undated account in the same volume. This one came from researcher Don Monroe who reported that three men had been out looking for a place to hunt elk when they spotted a large, hairy creature in the brush around Johnny Creek. The creek is in the north-central portion of the state in Phillips County. According to the witnesses, the creature was in a berry patch that contained a lot of huckleberries.

Bigfoot Through the Decades

1960s

Moving to the modern era of sightings in Montana, there's an abundance of encounters, many that include one of the elements missing in Bauman's tale—a visual sighting of the creature.

Bigfoot researcher John Green recalled doing an open-line radio show when a woman called in to report that there had been Bigfoot activity in the Snowy Mountains when she was a child. Reportedly, people in the region knew that cattle had to be kept at lower elevations in the late fall and early spring, otherwise "the hairy men that lived in the mountains would kill them and eat them."

The woman told Green that her father and a friend had seen one of the creatures in the area when she was growing up. Her uncle had also spotted one and intended to shoot it, but as soon as he reached for his gun, the Bigfoot ran away.

John Green's archives also contain a notation from the 1960s that Dr. Joseph Feathers from the Western Montana College of Education wrote that Dean Staton found bare human footprints in the snow 15 miles south of Jackson in Beaverhead County. The print that was measured came in at 17 inches in length and 9 inches in width. The creature appeared to have stepped over a four-foot-high windfall without breaking stride. The tracks continued for 300 yards to a rocky slope on the mountainside.

The men's magazines of the 1960s and 1970s frequently covered stories of giant hairy creatures. From the Himalayan Yeti to Bigfoot in the Pacific Northwest, the sensational aspects of the undiscovered creature made good headlines and feature articles.

Argosy, Saga, True, and others reported on sightings of the creature. One interesting account from Montana appeared in the January 1961 issue of *Saga* magazine in 1960 and involves a man named Roy W. Rye.

A Sasquatch was spotted near Seeley Lake in 1959.

Rye described an experience he'd had while bear hunting in the foothills of the Mission Mountains near Seeley Lake the previous year. It was December 1959 and Rye was following a set of tracks in the snow. While following the trail, he crossed a small clearing and suddenly felt that he wasn't alone. As reported in Saga:

"He looked around to his left and then to his right. There it was, twenty yards away, looking straight at him was this thing. Its head and arms were resting on a fallen tree that was five or six feet above the ground. Seeing only the head and arms, Rye thought it was a large bear, a very large bear. He began to raise his rifle to his shoulder. The thing, still looking at him, still leaning on the fallen tree, grinned at him—or so Rye thought. Then the thing let go an eerie, half-human scream. Its head began to rock from side to side and Rye could hear a rumbling sound. His rifle at the ready, Rye back-pedaled. The thing moved a moment and Rye could see it from the waist up. It had a large flat head, stubby ears, a short neck, and sloping shoulders with long arms. It was all covered with brownish grey hair."

The *Saga* article caught the attention of some Montana newspapers and publications. Reporters decided to follow up on the story and talk to Rye themselves. It seems at least some of the reporters were hoping to cast doubt on the tale, but the facts they discovered only added weight to the account.

The *Billings Gazette* found out that Rye had been a licensed game guide and had killed a lot of bears during his hunting career. Obviously, he wasn't someone apt to mistake what was or wasn't a bear.

The *Montana Sports Outdoors* magazine wrote about Rye in the publication's December 1960 issue, a month before the *Saga* article appeared. Writers with the outdoors magazine talked to Rye and got details of his account. He told the magazine, very firmly, that what he had seen was not a bear. Rye told reporters that he thought the creature looked "more like a huge ape." The magazine goes on:

"At the time, Rye was armed with a .270 rifle and a shoulder-holstered .357 magnum pistol. What did he do next? Why, he did what any other red-blooded, well-armed hunter would have done under the circumstances. He broke all records for cross country running in getting the heck out of there."

The *Daily Missoulian* also followed up on Rye's story and they too found that the man's facts checked out.

Researcher Greg Mastel sent a pair of interesting sightings to John Green involving 1960s encounters:

In November 1962, a Hamilton man named Reed Christenson saw a large bipedal creature running up an embankment. Christenson and his wife and daughter were near the top of Lost Trail Pass in Ravalli County when they spotted the thing. According to the witness, the creature was between six and seven feet tall, had long arms, and no neck. It was 2 a.m. when the family spotted the creature, and it likely didn't expect any humans to be in the area at that time of the morning.

It's also noted that the family's dog acted strangely during the sighting.

Another Hamilton man, Lou Bigley, spotted a hairy biped two years later. In August 1964, Bigley was hauling logs out of upper Grid Creek. His day soon took a strange turn. Driving along the road, he spotted a brown creature on two legs standing in the middle of the road about a hundred feet in front of his truck. Bigley said the creature was five feet tall with broad shoulders. The man slammed on the brakes, and the creature turned and ran up a rocky draw and out of sight.

Green's book, *Sasquatch: The Apes Among Us*, recounts a May 1964 sighting. Gray Simons and Sid Richardson took a group of Boy Scouts out camping at an area called Brown's Gulch near Butte. The scouts thought they were in for a nice, normal spring campout, but at about four o'clock in the morning, one of the boys was awakened by a noise outside his tent. The scout discovered a Sasquatch standing out front. He later said the creature was hairy all over with silver tipped brown hair. The creature also had a "heavy beard."

Shocked by the confrontation, the boy screamed, causing the Bigfoot to run away. Simons rushed to see what was happening. On investigation, the creature was heard nearby, splashing in the creek. Reportedly it was making "giggling sounds" similar to those a human would make. Perhaps it was amused that it had shocked the scout troop.

Tracks were discovered around the area the next morning. They appeared to be barefoot human tracks, but the size was exceptional—the prints were twenty inches long and six inches wide with a seven-foot stride. The trackway was clear for a hundred and fifty yards before the trail vanished in rocky strata.

Another group of Boy Scouts had an encounter with a large hairy man in the mid-'60s (original source of report unknown), About a dozen scouts were camped one night in the Deer Lodge National Forest in Silver Bow County when something intruded into their camp. As one of the boys who was present reports:

"The kid next to me heard something going through our backpacks, knocking things over. Then all of a sudden, this thing stepped on my friend. There was a lot of screaming.

"We turned our flashlights on it. It was dark brown, black. It walked like a man (and) took great big strides. (It) was three times my size—way over 8 feet tall. We saw it moving away across a ridge.

"There were numerous footprints going across the top of the ridge, bigger than anything I had ever seen before. They were human-like, with five toes (and) no claw marks."

Researcher Albert Rosales collected an account that occurred in 1964.

On August 11, 1964, a logger by the name of Lou Smalley encountered a five-foot-tall shaggy creature that was standing on a rugged point of rocks in the Girds Creek area near Hamilton. It was evening and Smalley was driving a logging truck when he spotted the Bigfoot. He elected to keep going rather than stop and look any closer at the creature.

In one of those synchronicities that make some researchers uncomfortable, the incident occurred at the same time as a couple named Ballew spotted a shiny object in the sky that emitted a strong light over the area.

A Montana associate sent me an account from 1965 involving a track find that puzzled a man named Bob Shook of Hamilton. Shook was out hunting at Piquett Creek south of Darby when he and several friends came across some five toed tracks that looked human but were so large that a man's arm from elbow to fingertip could fit inside one. The tracks were clearly impressed in soft dirt so there was no mistaking the size.

The incident was even more puzzling since they had heard what they thought was an animal "whistling" around their camp the previous night. They also smelled an overpowering odor although they could not find the source of either of the anomalies. The incidents bothered the men enough that they slept locked in their camper truck rather than outside in the open.

A few years later in the same area (exact date not given), another group of hunters had a weird experience. The men were in a camper when they saw "an ugly black round face" peering inside at them. Once they noticed it, the face disappeared, but seconds later the vehicle started rocking so hard they feared it was going to tip over.

On September 11, 1968, Harold Nelson was spending the night in his camper truck in Yellowstone County and had a frightening experience. The man wasn't too far from Billings when the incident occurred. Nelson was sitting quietly eating a can of beans when he became alarmed by loud noises outside his camper. He decided to investigate the commotion and, flashlight in hand, he opened the camper door only to receive the shock of his life—he was face to face with a Bigfoot. As reported in *Saga* magazine in the July 1969 issue:

"It had an ape-like face, but it was definitely not a gorilla." Nelson said later, "The head was slightly pointed, sloping down like the sketches of cavemen. The whole body was covered with reddish-brown hair. There were a few spots of white hair along the edge of the enormous shoulders. It stood erect, like a man, and must have weighed six hundred to eight hundred pounds. He was big—*real big*."

Frozen in fear the man stood looking at the creature. He reports that the thing made an odd noise, "sort of like a gargle and a whistle at the same time."

The situation changed, however, when the beast raised its arms up and reached toward the witness. The man's reaction was to scream as loud as he could. This time it was the Sasquatch who was shocked. The creature jumped back in surprise. The man thought the thing was frowning at his reaction. Not wasting time, the man leapt back inside his camper and grabbed a pistol to defend himself. He may have been expecting a full attack from the beast, but again, he was surprised at the behavior. He reports that the creature:

"Cocked his head in a funny motion and looked through the door. I sobbed with absolute relief when the beast turned away and shuffled back into the trees."

Researcher Roger Patterson, famous for the Patterson-Gimlin Bigfoot footage, received a letter from Great Falls resident Frank Zalenski who reported that he and another man, Bob Marshall, were out hunting in the region when they discovered a large footprint. Details are scant, but Zalenski reportedly placed his own foot in the print and the impression was three to four inches longer than his own foot. The incident occurred sometime in 1968, although the exact date was not given.

In the summer of 1969, a trio from Oregon were fishing a mile east of Bonner when their encounter occurred. Steve Filtcher saw what he initially thought was a bear but noticed that it had a face like a man. The figure walked like a human and had a manlike shape. It was brownish black in color and stood around eight feet tall. The incident, collected by John Green, also notes that Steve and his companions, Rose and Jerry Filtcher, all felt like they were being watched while they were at the fishing spot.

In 1969, Ted Foster was cutting lodge poles east of Lost Trail Pass when he started having the feeling that someone was walking behind him. He shut his power saw down and listened carefully. Turning around, he spotted a large creature not far away. The beast was described as a "seven foot, three-hundred-pound ape-man covered with black hair." The *Bitterroot Journal* reported the incident, adding:

"Thinking to defend himself, Ted started the saw. The creature didn't move, but the hair stood up on its neck. Ted turned the saw off, the hair on the animal's neck settled back down again. Without taking his eyes off Ted, the beast turned sideways and began walking away with huge, graceful steps... The incident occurred about 3 p.m. in broad daylight."

Foster commented that he thought the Bigfoot may have been investigating after hearing the sound of the chainsaw. Clearly, the creature did not like the noise.

Montana newshounds had their share of Bigfoot stories in the '60s and '70s and at least one reporter ended up getting much closer to the creature than he expected. Tom Tiede, a reporter for Kalispell's *Inter Lake*, had a weird encounter while on the trail of a completely different story.

His encounter took place sometime in the 1960s, though Tiede didn't write about it until much later so the exact date is not given. As he recalls, he was in a wooded area near Columbia Falls searching for a hermit who reportedly lived in the region. Tiede was having difficulty finding the hermit and sat down to rest before heading back out of the forest. His rest was cut short by a wailing sound that he described as rhythmic and patterned. "Happy wailing," he called it, noting its singsong quality.

The reporter became very worried that a group of hunters was in the area. Since he was not wearing red or orange to distinguish that he was a human, he fretted over the dangerous possibilities. Tiede considered calling out but quickly thought better of it. The "singsong" wailing continued, and he reached for his gun. Moments later, the source of the unusual sound became clear. As Tiede writes:

"Suddenly, and I swear by the Abominable Snowman, I saw it. About 50 yards away. Coming down off one of the interconnected hills, passing at a moderate speed through the woods, disappearing and reappearing in the trees. I don't remember feeling anything. I could see plainly that it was not like anything I had ever seen before. It had swinging arms, like a B-grade gorilla movie, a gray coat of hair, and a small head which I could not make out. And it was moving parallel to me."

The reporter wasn't sure whether or not the Bigfoot had in turn spotted him, but he had the impression that the creature looked in his direction.

"As it stopped, so did its song. I raised my rifle, forgot to take the safety off, but did nothing anyway. The thing paused for just a moment, then moved, silently now, off in a direction my shaky compass said was north.

"I beat it out of the forest then, and to hell with the old hermit, I never went back. I never wrote the story before either."

1970s

As the 1970s rolled in, sightings of large hairy bipeds were in abundance around the state. There were some unique aspects of encounters from this period. While some of the

56

reports were vague and brief (as is often the case with unknown creatures), others were rich in detail. Significantly, during the 1970s in Montana, many sightings were investigated by law enforcement officers who took the presence of unidentified creatures seriously.

The website Bigfootencounters.com lists a pair of incidents from the beginning of the decade:

In 1970, a group of people at a party at Crystal Lake in Kalispell found a set of footprints in the area. The prints measured eighteen inches and one foot appeared to be crippled. Similar prints were also found around a set of garbage cans in the area.

A year later, a man named Gary Huff discovered footprints in the same area. They were measured at seventeen inches. Huff tracked the prints over a ridge, then spotted a pair of hairy bipeds—they were walking hand in hand. Huff said one of the creatures was very large and the other one smaller. Both had hair all over their bodies.

Bigfoot sightings, along with other strange incidents such as cattle mutilations and UFO sightings, were investigated by officers with the Cascade County Sheriff's Office. John Green visited the officers and remarked how unusual it was for a sheriff to be involved in such investigations:

"After years of careful sparring with polite but skeptical policemen on the subject of hairy creatures, I found the reception at the Cascade County Sheriff's Office all but overwhelming. Captain Wolverton devoted a day to showing us around and Undersheriff Glenn Osborne was equally hospitable. What was really mind-blowing was being taken into a special room in the county building and shown on the wall a large map with reported sightings of hairy monsters (several more than I have mentioned) carefully plotted on it."

Not only was a county sheriff and his officers involved, but a publication was devoting a lot of space to the topic and they weren't laughing. Hamilton publication, the *Bitterroot Journal*, covered plenty of Bigfoot accounts, and did so without an agenda or insulting attitude.

John Green received a report that was apparently called in to police officers in Kalispell. An unnamed man was driving west of the city in September 1973 when his car was "run off the road by two large gorillas walking on hind legs."

Curiously, the same month, almost 130 miles away near Bonner, there was a series of other roadside encounters. According to Green's records, many motorists in the area said there was an ape throwing rocks off a cliff down at their vehicles.

According to the John Green archives, a woman near Kalispell was out walking her dogs in August 1974 when she came across two sets of tracks. Strangely, one set had three toes on the front part of the foot and the other was a 16 inch, five-toed track. When the larger one went uphill, it became three-toed. The woman's dogs reportedly went wild in the area, likely from the scent they picked up.

Bitterroot wilderness

Marian T. Place's *Bigfoot All Over the Country* reports on a September 1974 incident in the Bitterroot Mountains:

A group of five university students were out for a hike at St. Mary's Peak, thirty miles west of Missoula. A variety of marked trails offers paths ranging from moderate to steep at the location. Two of the men went straight for the top, but a third man, Chris Tobias, opted to take it easy due to a recent knee operation. Two women followed behind him wanting to take their time and not rush up the trail.

At midafternoon, Tobias turned off the trail to rest his aching knee. He sat down on a rocky ledge and took in the view of the mountainside. While taking in the scenery, he noticed two figures come out of the trees below him. As he watched, he noticed the figures were moving at a rapid pace, much quicker than the average human. And in fact, as they began to get closer, Tobias realized they weren't human at all. The bipedal creatures were black and hairy and were moving in a very smooth fashion. Once they were less than a hundred yards away, they turned down a ravine and were out of sight.

Trying to calm himself and understand what he had witnessed, the man was surprised when two of his hiking companions rushed up and exclaimed "Chris! We saw something really weird walking along that ridge below you."

Diane Stringen and Kathy Mudd, the two female hikers, had watched the creatures from their vantage point and realized they were seeing something unusual. As Kathy reported:

"We saw they were hairy all over! They weren't human! They were those Bigfoot creatures we've read about."

Greg Mastel reported that a family having a party near Rattlesnake Creek outside of Missoula in 1974 heard loud screams outside. When they investigated, they discovered footprints measuring eighteen inches in the area. The grandfather told his family that such occurrences had been frequent in the area for many years.

Keith Wolverton—that's the same Wolverton who was a Cascade County Sheriff—wrote a book about some of the weird cases he investigated. The book, *Mystery Stalks the Prairie*, is a treasure trove of weird accounts including a number of Bigfoot sightings. Wolverton reports on a December 1974 account from a Great Falls man who took some shots at a Bigfoot.

The man was coyote hunting on Bootlegger Trail when he saw the creature that he said was seven or eight feet tall and looked like a grizzly bear. The hunter fired his .30-30 at the creature, but it advanced on him anyway, causing him to rush to his car and leave the scene.

Mrs. Presley Lay and her son, along with his wife and children, saw a creature in the fall of 1974. The group were near the Bitterroot River when they spotted the Bigfoot about 200 yards from their position. The creature was covered in brown hair, walked upright and swung its arms in an "exaggerated fashion" as it moved quickly from one side of a clearing to the opposite side. The account was sent to John Green.

The Cascade County Sheriff's office received a report on December 26, 1975, from a pair of frightened junior high school girls. The first girl, a resident of Great Falls, was spending the Christmas holidays with a second girl who lived on a horse property outside of Vaughn.

Late in the afternoon, the girls noticed that the horses were in an agitated state, stamping the ground, rearing up on their hind legs, and acting erratically. The girls quickly discovered the source of the horses' agitation: a figure about seven and a half feet tall was about two hundred yards away from the property's mobile home, and about 25 yards away from a thicket. As recounted in *Mystery Stalks the Prairie*:

"The Great Falls girl found a .22 rifle belonging to her friend's father and looked through the scope at the creature. She described its face as 'dark and awful-looking and not like a human's.' The girls said the creature was seven to seven and a half feet tall and twice as wide as a man."

Hoping to frighten the creature away, the girl fired the rifle into the air, but the hairy thing didn't react. She waited a short time, then fired again. Although the girl had not fired toward the creature, it seemed to behave as if it had been shot at, or even shot. In a bizarre display, the thing fell to the ground and started to pull itself along with its arms. After covering a short distance, it stood back up.

The two girls had seen enough. They turned on their heels and retreated from the area. When they looked back to see what the creature was doing, they spotted "three or four other creatures" helping the first biped get into the cover of some bushes.

Captain Wolverton was impressed by the report, and the obvious fright displayed by the girls served to reinforce that they were not lying or trying to pull a prank. The girls also volunteered to take a polygraph test, and both of them passed.

The night after the incident, Captain Wolverton, Undersheriff Glen Osborne, and Deputy Dick Gasvoda, went to the area of the sighting and conducted their own search for the creatures. Wolverton used a starlight scope to scan the area and the other men went into the brush to try to flush out anything lurking out of sight.

While the officers didn't spot any Bigfoot in the area, they did find a number of tree breaks that were unusual and similar to those found at other reported sighting locations.

The officers also spoke with the Vaughn girl's father who related his own tale. The man told the law men that shortly after midnight on Christmas morning, he was awakened by a sound he described as "like a human dying an agonizing death."

The man took a flashlight and went outside to investigate. While the witness acted bravely, his dog did not and refused to go outside.

Apparently, he either failed to find anything or retreated back inside. Whatever the case, Wolverton doesn't note any further information about the incident.

The captain himself returned to the property again the following day and walked around the area hoping to find footprints but discovered nothing.

The unsettling sound heard by the Vaughn witness was also reported by other people in the area. The following month, a man living just a few miles west of the property reported the same disturbing sound. Just like the Vaughn girl's father, the man noticed that his dogs, who were normally aggressive, were acting afraid, standing up against the house, and making very faint barking noises.

Echoing the Vaughn man's report, the witness also said the

scream was like that of a man dying in pain. The noise lasted about five minutes.

In February 1976, a resident of Babb called the sheriff's department to report that she and her husband had heard the weird sound the previous summer. While it's unclear why the woman waited so long to report the sounds, it's notable that the pattern was the same, a miserable moaning echoing in the night and dogs that acted terrified. According to *Mystery Stalks the Prairie*:

She said other residents of Babb had heard the sound, too, and she understood a man from Browning had seen "Bigfoot" on Logan Pass in Glacier Park the preceding summer. Authorities did not have the man's name so they could not check the story.

On February 11, 1976, Captain Wolverton received a report from an airman who said he had found bipedal tracks near Beaver Creek, in the Rocky Mountains. According to the airman, the creature that left the tracks had three toes.

Heavy snowfall prevented Wolverton from investigating the scene closely, but he did fly over the area hoping to see something from the air. He reported nothing unusual.

Not long after the two girls had their weird encounter, a pair of boys in Ulm, a few miles southwest of Great Falls, had a sighting. It was February 21, 1976, and the boys were near a bridge that crossed over the Missouri River. One of the young men saw a hair-covered arm reaching out from some bushes. The second boy, who was farther ahead on the trail, saw a tall creature with dark brown hair and "glowing whitish-yellow eyes."

The boys reported the incident to the sheriff's department, but it was more than two weeks after the sighting, so officers felt it was pointless to investigate the site. The boys were given polygraph tests, and both passed.

Something must have stirred the creatures up that week because the following morning, East Helena resident Leonard Hegele was traveling on Interstate 15 south of Great Falls International Airport when he spotted a large bipedal creature moving across a field around a quarter of a mile from the highway.

Hegele stopped the car and got out with a .357 magnum in hand. He ran into the field to pursue the creature and got within 700 feet of it, but when it turned and faced him, he decided to retreat to his vehicle.

Hegele told Cascade County sheriff's officers that the hairy thing was seven feet tall with three-foot-wide shoulders. His wife and children were with him at the time of the sighting.

Also, in February '76, a young man named Leonard Semgard had a fright when he was on his way home from school one afternoon. The thirteen-year-old boy usually walked through a field on his route, but on this particular day, the field was occupied by an eight-foot-tall creature covered in dark hair. The boy rushed to a phone booth and called his grandmother to come retrieve him.

The following month, on March 7, a woman phoned and spoke with a deputy sheriff to report a creature sighting. She said the thing was crossing a road on the highway north of Vaughn when she spotted it. It was reddish-brown and hairy. The woman said the beast was standing in a ditch with one arm forward. She had the impression it was about to cross the road.

Later that month, a teenager said he saw a hairy creature standing in the middle of Dempsey Road in Great Falls. The boy was riding his bike around nine o'clock at night. The creature ran through a hedge in the yard of a house and vanished. Like many other witnesses of the period, the boy was given a polygraph test and passed.

The following month, another young man spotted a tall hairy creature near his home in Helena. According to Captain Wolverton and Deputy Ken Anderson, who investigated the case, the boy woke up around 4:30 AM on April 4 because he was restless. He stood in his room, looking out his second story window where he had a good view of the pasture to the east of his home. At around 5 AM, the boy spotted "a tall hairy creature walking in the pasture, coming from the south, or right."

The boy estimated the creature at about eight feet in height and told the officers that it moved with long strides while its arms went back and forth as a human's would. The boy provided the officers further details of the thing's appearance; according to their report:

"Creature did not appear to have a neck, but it was capable of turning its head and it appeared to be looking around. Except for its face, it was covered entirely with brown or black hair about an inch to an inch and a half long."

The boy could not describe the creature's face, but said the nose appeared "pushed in." He also reported that the thing's forehead protruded out, then upward to a rounded head.

The witness said the creature's movement was very smooth and that it did not appear to bend its knees very much as it walked. The creature's arms were thick and there was no visible curve in the small of the thing's back.

As the boy watched the hairy beast, it moved directly east of the house where it was joined by another, smaller creature. The witness reported that the second creature was the same color as the first, but about a head shorter.

Oddly, the larger creature reached down and picked up a dark colored object "about the size of a bale of hay," with something flapping on the ends that "looked similar to a piece of dark plastic."

As the boy observed, the larger creature passed the item over to the smaller figure, then they continued toward the house. The creature came to within about a hundred feet of the boy's home at which point it appeared to look directly toward the young man's window.

The frightened boy rushed downstairs and reported the incident to his father. By the time the boy managed to get his father to the window, the creatures had disappeared.

The following day, the young man's sister found a track in the pasture and she and her brother covered it with wood until the next day when they made a plaster cast of it.

Officers Wolverton and Anderson were impressed by the young man's testimony and noted that the boy was upset over being misquoted in the newspaper where it was reported that he had claimed the initial creature was ten feet tall. The boy drew sketches of what he saw and gave them to the officers.

The officers made their own cast of the track find and discovered that it was three toed, 17 ½ inches long, and 7 inches wide.

Apparently, the property was quite a hotspot for Bigfoot activity. While speaking with the boy's father, deputies learned about another incident twelve days prior to the boy's sighting.

The boy's father reported that he had been taking a bath when he heard noises outside the bathroom window. He got dressed and went outside to investigate, and he discovered a large footprint in the snow outside the window. He reported that there were also other scratch marks on either side of the print.

Wolverton and Anderson soon found that the whole family had stories to share. The boy's mother reported that a range of strange things had been occurring around the property. She reported hearing what sounded like heavy running outside the house, and she told officers that the family dogs had been acting frightened. Additionally, the family was hearing weird sounds they described as somewhere between an elk bugling and dogs howling. Even more bizarre is a note regarding other tracks in the area, as reported in *Mystery Stalks the Prairie*:

"As officers searched the pasture area where the two creatures were seen, they noticed both cattle tracks and horse prints. When they asked the boy's father when the horses were taken out to pasture, he replied, 'There's never been horses in that pasture.'"

Three-toed creatures, phantom horses—what exactly was taking place at the property? As far as the sheriff's office was concerned, the reports were valid though unexplained. Wolverton's official report stated: "After talking to (the boy) and his family, I believe that (the boy) did see what he reported."

Another incident reported to me by a correspondent details a July 1976 sighting. A woman and her daughter watched a hairy creature for a half an hour in Pfeiling Gulch. The women had driven up a remote logging road and were out picking berries when the daughter noticed the biped several hundred yards away. She described the creature as around eight feet tall with straw colored hair on its head and shoulders, and dark brown hair on the rest of its body.

The thing was clearly watching the women and as it did, it moved its head from side to side. As the women observed, the creature's head movements stopped, and it stood still. Finally, it sat down, keeping its attention on the two women.

The daughter was curious and wanted to get a better look, so she started walking toward the Bigfoot. She didn't get far before she lost her nerve and backtracked. The women got back in their car and left the area.

The *Great Falls Tribune* mentioned another incident that occurred in July '76 five miles from Great Falls. A female motorist traveling at 5:30 a.m. on I-15 saw a hairy biped standing near the great Knoll on the Freeway about twenty feet away.

The creature was between seven and eight feet in height and covered in dark brown or black hair. The woman was shocked by the sight and stopped her vehicle as she watched the creature walk away to the west. Curiously, the same day a 7.9 earthquake struck central Montana. Was the creature on the move that day because of the earthquake? Some researchers have noted a correlation between earthquake activity and Bigfoot sightings. Perhaps, like other animals, they are sensitive to pending quake activity.

A report from July 21, 1976, came from four men who said they saw a pair of bipedal hairy creatures walking along a hill toward the Rainbow Dam. The brief incident was noted in the *Great Falls Tribune* in its July 31 edition.

The vague report was one of many in 1976, a busy year for Montana's mystery creatures. In October, Gail Kapptie of the Vaughn area had a sighting of an eight-foot-tall beast that appeared to be raiding her chicken coop.

Kapptie and her son had found the gate of a sheep pen opened during the day and eighteen-inch prints around the pen. The prints were human-like but had only four toes. Grain had also disappeared from one of Kapptie's storage bins, so it was clear that something was treating the Kapptie farm as a buffet.

The woman was alerted by her dog barking that night which led to her seeing the creature. She described it as "tall, tan and ape-like with very long arms." When the creature realized Kapptie was watching it, it ran away at high speed.

The Oregonbigfoot.com website mentions a September 1976 sighting from Silver Bow County involving yet another group of Boy Scouts. In this case, some scouts on a bus spotted a tall, hairy creature running behind some bushes before it vanished into a logging area. The creature also reportedly had a horrible smell.

The sighting took place near Browns Gulch Boy Scout camp in Butte.

Another account sent to me reports that an unidentified game guide and two clients hunting in the Tobacco Root Mountains in October 1976 reportedly saw a pair of Bigfoots that stood eight to nine feet tall. The creatures were in a clearing about 100 yards from the men. Both creatures were coal black in color, but one had a white streak on its back.

In Sasquatch: The Apes Among Us, John Greene includes a brief note about three men near Gerber in Cascade County who spotted a Bigfoot in April 1977. The creature was 6 ½ feet tall and covered in thick, black hair that was about four inches long. The men decided to chase the creature. It initially ran but then turned to face the men. Purportedly, the men stood their ground and drove the creature off.

The Anomaly Research Bulletin (number 8), reported that a pair of campers saw three Bigfoots near Silver City, Lewis and Clark County, in June 1977. The creatures were a staggering ten feet tall.

A BFRO entry reports that a man out doing some night fishing in August 1977 ended up sharing some of his catch with a Sasquatch, but it wasn't by choice.

Hauser Dam in Lewis & Clark County.

The man was fly-fishing along the Missouri River near Hauser Dam in Lewis and Clark County. He used some rocks and formed a small, circular pool near the water's edge to hold the fish he caught. It was after eleven o'clock and very dark, so the man placed a light on a boulder and continued fishing about twenty yards upstream of the light. He realized he had lost the fly off his line and headed back to the light to get a new one. As he approached the boulder, he noticed movement around the area and used his light to get a look at what he was dealing with. He received quite a surprise:

"I was starting to hear a crackling sound and see movement from the brush. I pointed the beam directly at the movement only 10 feet from me and got a full view of a hairy bipedal creature moving very rapidly up the bank and quartering away from me in the downstream direction. It was very large and muscular with long dark hair and seemingly no neck. Estimated height is about 7-8 feet, guessing 400-500 pounds. I could not see its face as it was moving away from me. It took long, powerful strides and its arms moved powerfully as a man would move walking very rapidly. It was amazing to see how quickly it traversed over the boulders and up the steep embankment. I had the creature in the lamp beam for only a few seconds before it disappeared into the darkness."

When the shocked fisherman turned to check on his catch, he received another surprise:

"Before the sighting of the creature, I had four trout ranging from 2 to 3 pounds in the pool. After the sighting, there were only two trout…the creature must have been foraging along the river's edge and found an easy meal."

The man took the remaining fish and his gear and headed out of the area.

Sasquatch: The Apes Among Us mentions a report from the same year. On August 20, Staff Sergeant Fred Wilson of Malmstrom Air Force Base reported that he and a group of boys he had taken out into the wilderness spotted a Bigfoot. Wilson said the group spotted "A 15-foot creature on a ridge in Belt Creek Canyon."

The incident occurred at two in the morning. Heavy rain had moved into the area, leading the group to break camp. They were on their way to their vehicles when they heard noises that attracted their attention. By flashlight beam they saw a large, hairy creature standing near a clump of bushes. According to Wilson, the thing was: "Covered with long hair, having no neck, standing on two legs."

It was Wilson who estimated the extremely large height of fifteen feet. One member of the party grabbed a shotgun and fired two shots in the creature's direction as the thing started running toward them. They made it into their cars and fled the scene. Wilson later took a polygraph test and passed.

Around the same time, but farther west on the outskirts of Missoula, a young girl out horseback riding had a daytime encounter with a Bigfoot.

The girl was riding in a wooded area bordering the Rattlesnake Wilderness. It was a peaceful summer ride until both the girl and her horse were startled by something unusual. As she recalls:

"My horse stopped dead in its tracks as we rode through a meadow. There I was, face to face with a Bigfoot that was about 10 feet away from me. It was peeking out from behind a tree.

It just stood there looking at me and didn't make a sound. I slowly turned my horse around and ran home. It must have stood at least 7 feet or more taller than myself. That was the only time I witnessed one."

The woman reported her sighting years later (1997) to the BFRO (Bigfoot Field Researchers Organization). She adds a note to the 1997 statement that indicates activity still continues in the region:

"As of today, my husband and myself built a home on the Clark Fork River on the outskirts of Missoula, MT, and over the last two summers we heard an odd sort of scream that sounds almost like a prehistoric bird, really gravelly, and it travels very fast, covering a lot of ground. This sound has only happened in the summertime, usually right before daybreak, or right after midnight.

"The neighbors have heard it, but no one can figure it out! It kind of sends chills down your spine, and all the neighbor dogs start to bark like in your tape recordings." [the witness was indicating recordings of purported Bigfoot sounds on the BFRO website].

The witness also added that her grandparents had spotted a Bigfoot thirty years previously. The couple saw the creature running through a river bottom near their home in the Swan Valley. "They said it looked like a hairy man loping through the brush of the river bottom that ran in front of their home," she said.

Apparently, Boy Scouts in Montana have a high probability of encountering a Sasquatch because yet another troop of scouts spotted one in July 1978 in Lewis and Clark County. According to the brief report given to me, a Jamboree was being held near the town of Helena and two young scouts spotted one of the creatures at the edge of the river. The beast was described as "gorilla-like and about 6 feet tall."

The two boys observed the creature picking leaves off a bush and eating them. After a few moments, the Bigfoot walked into the trees and disappeared.

Unfortunately, no further details were provided, nor was

the original source of the account reported to me.

A hunting trip in the fall of 1978 resulted in a Bigfoot sighting in Madison County near Virginia City. The witness recalled the sighting in a BFRO report and says he and his cousin, along with his father and uncle, were out for an early morning hunt on October 21, the opening day of deer season. The reporting witness and his cousin were riding in the back of a pickup truck as the group made its way up Alder Gulch. The pair was scanning the area looking for deer. On their right was a hillside meadow covered with thigh-high sage brush. They spotted what they first thought was another hunter but quickly realized that the figure was in all black, something a hunter would never do. Looking at the figure, they realized it was an animal and they knew what they were observing. As the witness recounts:

"Make no bones about it, the animal had the distinctive dome-shaped head with no neck, broad shoulders, and was solid black. The animal was facing us and slightly bent forward and looked as if it was resting its right arm on its right knee. It occurred to me that he/she knew it got caught out in the open and was just going to stay motionless and hoped we would drive right by. The closest tree line was about 50 yards away from the Bigfoot and it had taken us only about 15 seconds to get back to where we could see the sage brush meadow again."

The witness later stated that the figure had "no neck" and both men recall the incident to this day. The witness added:

"I have hunted most of my life and have seen most animals that live in these woods. My cousin has been hunting all his life and knows every animal there is in these woods as well. We will never forget that morning and we talk about it with each other occasionally."

Kalispell's *Weekly News* reported an incident in June 1979 involving two men who told Whitefish police that they had found tracks in a streambed. A group of officials, including a game warden, a forest ranger, and a police officer, went out to investigate the report. The men found three clear prints on a sand bar, several others on a gravel bank, and more in a nearby pasture. The tracks were 17 inches in length, 9 inches wide, and showed a stride of almost five feet.

The game warden estimated that the creature was in the neighborhood of 700 pounds. A plaster cast was made and sent to a scientist at the University of Montana.

In the winter of 1979, a motorist on Highway 200 saw a light-colored Sasquatch crossing the road late one night. The witness told the BFRO:

"What has to be a Bigfoot crossed the road in front of me at the end of the guard rails, headed north. He was well over six feet tall; he didn't even turn his head to look at me, he just walked across the road...his hair was not extremely long or matted, but light colored and the wind was whipping through it and it was darker at the skin than at the tips."

The sighting occurred at around 11:30 at night and temps were below zero.

1980s

In 1982, a group of young men out riding horses on the Blackfeet Reservation in Glacier County had a Bigfoot encounter preceded by a warning from their horses. Charles K. Wolftail reported the incident, and it was posted on Bigfootencounters. com.

The men had been riding most of the day, and with evening approaching, they had turned for home. As they approached the trailhead, one of the horses was reluctant and fought the bridle. The men pushed on and once they were well in the brush, their horses started behaving oddly, stepping softly, and snorting as if bothered by a scent. As the reporting witness states:

"Our horses began jumping in different directions like they were scared of something. The first thing on all our minds was a bear! We began looking in different directions trying to find the location of the bear.

"I don't remember who was the first to sight what we saw. I just heard him swear and ask the rest of us to look. We all looked in the direction he was pointing and saw this very tall thing running on two legs beside us and then it turned in front of us. The thing crossed the trail in front of us about 40 feet and stopped at the edge of the brush. It just stared at us as if in the same amount of amazement as we were, and then it disappeared into the trees just as fast."

The witness described the creature as the hairiest man he had ever seen and well over six feet tall. The party returned to the spot the following day and found branches broken off at six to eight feet high in the area where they had seen the creature. They also found footprints, though no size was indicated in the report.

Another BFRO report details a sighting from the summer of 1982 from Lewis and Clark County. Some teenage boys were near the town of Lincoln staying at a cabin when the incident unfolded. As the reporting witness states:

"I felt as if we were being watched. The hair on the back of my neck even stood up. We heard something in the woods ahead of us. The noise stopped, and we continued back towards the cabin. About 400 yards from the cabin, I looked toward the wood line, and I saw a figure standing up and looking at us."

The creature was black in color and at least six feet tall. The boys found a massive footprint in the area two days later. The reporting witness states that he wears a size twelve shoe, but the print was four to six inches longer and a lot wider than his foot.

The boys had a second sighting as they were walking back to the cabin. One boy noticed something in the woods and pointed to the area:

"I finally saw what he saw. Sitting on an old tree stump was what I believe to be a Bigfoot. We were only 50 yards away from him, and I could see clearly. It sat there looking at us.

It looked in another direction while we were staring at it, and it was like he did not have a neck. He moved his whole upper torso, and then looked back at us. When he did this, we took off running."

A Montana correspondent told me about an incident from

June 9, 1985. Reportedly, three hikers saw an ape-like creature fording a river in waist deep water. The sighting was near Kalispell in Flathead County.

An encounter posted on Oregonbigfoot.com comes from a witness who spotted a Bigfoot in the Hamilton area of Ravalli County in 1986 (no exact date given). The witness watched as the creature came out of the woods and approached a salt lick that had been placed out for deer. According to the witness:

"He appeared to sniff it and then pulled it out of the ground and threw it. It was thrown three car-lengths with a 100-pound cement block on the bottom."

The reporting witness's grandfather retrieved a .22 rifle and started shooting at the creature, but it had no effect. As the report states:

"The thing just stood there as if he was shaking them off and then made a whiney noise and calmly walked back into the woods."

Bigfoot researcher Bobbie Short received an account from Audrey Dibble of Walkerville, Silver Bow County, involving incidents at Bull Run Gulch in 1988.

Dibble reports that the tracks of two Bigfoot creatures were found around the ranch that her son and his family were renting at the time.

Dibble's daughter-in-law had hiked a mile up into the gulch the day before the tracks were found and this seemed to attract the attention of the creatures. When the family backtracked the Bigfoot trail, they found that the creatures had followed the woman's track to the ranch.

The larger set of tracks circled around the house and barn and into the fields below the home. The smaller creature stayed near the rabbit hutches. It's noted in the reports that the smaller creature's tracks were "curled."

The large prints measured 17 inches in length while the smaller prints came in at 14 ½ inches long. Dibble reports:

"We took pictures of the prints and the thing that struck us most about the prints was that the creatures had to have been massive as it was very cold and the snow and ice on the ground was frozen so hard that we could jump up and down without breaking through to ground, but every print of both creatures went completely through the ice."

The following week, horrible screams were heard near the ranch. Dibble adds:

"At about midnight my daughter-in-law called me in a panic and said there was a horrible screaming coming through the trees on the other side of the fields and that she didn't think anything human could sound so guttural or masculine or angry."

A report posted on the BFRO website details an incident from May 1989 in Park County. Two people were out climbing on the west side of the Crazy Mountains and went to a timbered spot at about 7000' elevation. The flat-topped buttress had one juniper about 4-5' high.

As the hikers were returning down to their car, the reporting witness turned and looked back at the spot they had left.

"I was surprised to see that in addition to the lone tree there was another dark form that was swaying back and forth. I thought to myself, 'That's cool, there's a bear up there.' Then the 'bear' stood up and walked off the flat area down into a small rocky notch and up some steep rocks, then disappeared into the timber. It appeared to cover the distance in about 4-5 strides with very fluid motion."

The reporting witness notes that both he and his companion had the sensation of the hair going up on the backs of their necks when they witnessed the "bear." Additionally, the witness's friend had a mix breed dog on the hike and the animal acted strangely, growling and generally on guard while they were in the area.

Another pair of witnesses experienced a hair-raising feeling, not because of a sighting, but because of weird vocalizations heard around their property.

In the summer of 1989, two brothers on the Flathead reservation heard strange vocalizations near their family residence, about twenty miles NW of Missoula. According to the BFRO report, the incident occurred in the late afternoon on a July day.

The reporting witnesses said his brother came rushing to him and alerted him that he had heard something unusual in the woods around their home. The man describes the noises:

"I had heard a lot of strange sounds growing up in the deep woods over the years (elk mating calls, ruffed grouse beating their wings, coyotes, etc.), but never anything like this. I can't really describe the sound except that it was a high-pitched tone from a living thing that was very resonant, powerful, and well-controlled in its execution. It made the hair stand up on the back of my neck."

The brothers rushed to where the family dogs were and observed that the animals were looking into the woods, in the direction the sounds had come from, and barking. "I had never seen them barking like this, not even at bears," the witness reported.

In short order, the creature's vocalizations were answered

by another, similar creature:

"Whatever was out there, there seemed to be two of them and they seemed to be communicating. We continued to listen. Nothing for a minute or two. Then we heard two more distinct calls, this time from the same general direction in the woods yet separated. They were now coming from a farther distance. Again, they seemed to be replying or communicating to one another."

At the end of the report, the witness adds an interesting anecdote:

"I had another experience with a close friend the following year (1990) involving what we believed were Bigfoot tracks. When we told her about the incident, my friend's grandmother, who is in her late eighties and had lived in the location where we saw the tracks her whole life, relayed a story about how she and her husband had seen a Sasquatch in that area over 20 years ago." (Meaning around 1970)

1990s

A man in the Libby area of Lincoln county saw a trio of Bigfoots in January 1990 while he was walking his dog in the woods behind his home. The report comes via Ray Crowe's *Bigfoot Behavior Volume III*.

The man said the thing was a "human-like animal." The witness was alerted to the Bigfoot's presence after hearing footsteps behind him. He turned and spotted the creature about 100 yards from his position. He watched as the creature made its way across a field. The man's dog ran back to the house, presumably afraid of the Bigfoot, and the man followed suit. As he was headed back to his home, he saw two more hairy bipeds running across the field. He also reports hearing the creatures emit a screeching howl.

In 1990, Bigfoot hit the front page of The *Billings Gazette* when the paper reported on sightings occurring on the Fort Peck Reservation. According to the July 24 edition of the paper, residents in the Fort Kipp area of the Reservation were worried about the creature's presence. Indian Affairs officers spoke to the paper about the sightings:

"'Everybody is kind of keeping their eyes open,' said Glenn Littlebird, agency special officer. 'People around here are taking it seriously,' he said. 'They're kind of scared because, you know, that certain type of creature has been sighted around that area numerous times.'"

Theresa Buckelk, of Fort Kipp, claimed she spotted one of the hairy men running along U.S. Highway 2. She said the creature was more than six feet tall and ran on two legs. It crossed the highway and ran into the bush as the woman observed it. Buckelk also smelled a strong, foul odor when the creature was nearby.

Law enforcement officers from both Roosevelt County and the BIA (Bureau of Indian Affairs), investigated the scene but found no prints or other evidence of the hairy man's presence. The paper noted:

"Fred Steele of the Indian Health Service said he grew up hearing stories about Bigfoot, so he interviewed several people in the area and believes the creature is Bigfoot. 'People in that area had heard strange noises during the night before the creature was sighted,' Steele said."

The BFRO received a report about a Ravalli County encounter that took place in September 1991. The reporting witness in this case was an experienced big game hunting guide who recalls:

"Coming down a game trail on a ridge in deep dark timber. My horse was tired. All of a sudden, he became nervous. A little breeze coming to me. Went about 75 yards and my horse started looking to the left. About 25 to 30 feet there was a big root ball from a downed pine tree; from the waist up, crouching down, was a Bigfoot. I looked at him in the eyes. It was surprised as I. It was not an ape; it looked more like a man, but it had hair all over about 6 to 8 inches long. I had a rifle, but I was so close to it I was afraid to make any sudden moves other than just keep riding. I will never forget and some day if funds are available, I would like to make an effort to find it again."

BFRO investigator John Salmond followed up on the

report and had a phone conversation with the witness. Salmond gleaned a few other details from speaking with the man: the Bigfoot had reddish brown hair that covered its body. The facial hair was thin and did not cover the entire face. Skin was brownish and the face was more like a man than an ape. The witness believes the creature was male since no breasts were visible. The Bigfoot was large with 35-40-inch-wide shoulders. Height could not be determined because the creature was crouching behind the root ball during the sighting.

Salmond found the witness credible and points out that the man's extensive experience as a game guide has made him familiar with a wide range of large animals in the region.

Three people hiking in the Gallatin National Forest in the summer of 1993 saw a massive creature running through the woods. It was June 3, and the trio was in the Portal Creek area late in the day. Concerned about an incoming storm, they decided to "double time" down the west side of a windy pass so they could make it back to their vehicle before foul weather came in.

They heard something that was a distinct sound and not part of the wind that was blowing, something they thought was a howl. When they reached a clearing, they again heard what the reporting witness described as a howl that sent a chill up his spine. Moments, later, the hikers saw the creature that had apparently issued the sound. The witness described the moment in a BFRO entry:

"Something massive and dark and clearly running on two legs ran through the brush about sixty yards away and disappeared into the forest. I don't think any of us moved or spoke for about five minutes until we heard the howl (yell?) again (this time pretty far off and in the opposite direction than we were heading). We got out of there in a hurry."

The July 1996 edition of the *Montana Standard* reported on the discovery of 14-inch footprints that were cast by researchers Shannon Kelly and Kelly Cundiff northwest of Helena. The pair said the tracks were discovered west of Canyon Creek.

The researchers were drawn to the area after a number

of reports led them to believe a Sasquatch was in the region. According to the paper:

"It seems that last year, miners familiar with the forest and most of the things living in it heard screams in the night unlike the sound of any animal they had heard before, Kelly said.

"So, on the Fourth of July, Kelly headed into the area in search of whatever had spooked the miners. On Friday, Cundiff joined him in his search.

"Then, on Sunday afternoon, Cundiff spotted what the two had been looking for—a large print embedded in the hard soil, he said."

The prints were described as "ape-like" and something had pulled up plants in the area. Kelly estimated the weight of the creature that left the tracks to be about four hundred pounds. The pair planned to return to the site, and Kelly himself told the paper he would be in and out of the area throughout the summer.

Ray Crowe's *Bigfoot Behavior Volume II* lists an interesting sighting from 1997 involving an Immigration Service employee.

Eldon Garvis was at the US/Canadian border, 27 miles north of Havre on Highway 33, the Saint Joe Road, when he spotted a Bigfoot in a roadside ditch. Garvis's sighting was somewhere between the 1-15 of February, and it was around 12:30 a.m.

Garvis saw the creature as he passed by and estimated its height between five and six feet. It was covered with hair and was black in color. Garvis returned to the scene later and found three-toed tracks in the snow. It was clear from the tracks that the creature had turned around and retreated back into the field that it had come from. Garvis speculated that his vehicle's approach had frightened the beast away.

Reportedly, a lone hunter out in Cascade County in May 1995 spotted an eight-foot-tall creature that had glowing eyes. The thing had reddish brown hair, but no further description was offered. Apparently frightened, or startled, or both, the hunter fired at the creature and when he did so, the thing vanished in a flash of light. Researcher Linda Moulton Howe recounted the incident on the June 18, 1995, edition of the Art Bell Show.

Glacier National Park.

In *Where the Footprints End: Volume II,* authors Joshua Cutchin and Timothy Renner report an encounter from Glacier National Park.

The incident occurred on July 30, 1997. The witness, Travis, was working for the park doing maintenance and cleanup. He and another unnamed park employee were dispatched to clean a campsite area in the park and encountered a horrible, overpowering smell described as "like a dead skunk."

Continuing up the trail, one of the men exclaimed "Oh my God! There's a Bigfoot!"

The pair saw the creature lying on its side, tearing into a rotting tree. The loud exclamation from the witness alerted the creature and it jumped to its feet. Travis reports that he felt instantly nauseated.

The park radio that the men carried suddenly crackled

with static which apparently upset the Bigfoot because it started shaking all over, then let out a "ferocious roar." This was enough for the two witnesses who promptly fled the scene.

Reportedly, Travis was advised by some employees of the Forest Service to keep quiet about his encounter, telling him that no one would believe him and that others would make fun of him. Travis ignored the advice, shared his encounter, and started asking other park employees questions about Bigfoot.

The bizarre twist in the story—according to Travis, a federal agent showed up in a black Ford Explorer to intimidate him for asking questions and talking about Bigfoot.

Bigfoot researcher Bobbie Short received a report in June 1998 that strange, five-inch tracks had been found along the Blackfoot River. There's speculation that this was evidence of a juvenile Bigfoot, but unfortunately no further details are available.

An entry on the BFRO website recounts a July 1999 roadside sighting of an upright, hairy creature. The reporting witness and a friend were traveling east on US 90 in Park County when they saw a large, reddish-brown creature walking on the side of the road. Danny, the reporting witness, writes:

"It was very large. I don't know exactly how big or how much it could have weighed, but I do know the hands of the animal hung to about the tops of the fence posts it was walking next to. Those posts are about 3 to 4 feet of exposed post. There were two of us who saw the creature walking."

It was about 7:30 in the morning when the sighting occurred, and the creature was in clear view about 100 to 150 yards away from the witnesses.

In a follow up interview, Danny clarified that there were other passengers in the van, but only one other person was awake, and he also saw the creature Danny reported.

Flag of the Crow Nation

2000s

In the summer of 2001, rancher Steve Kukowski found himself the subject of a rumor that he had shot and killed a Bigfoot on his property at Pryor Creek.

"The rumors have been going on all summer. I have no idea what it is. I have no idea how it got started," Kukowski told the *Billings Gazette*. The October 23 report noted that the story had been circulating for three months and that there were different versions of the tale.

In some variations the creature was hit with a vehicle. Most versions indicated the Crow Reservation as the location of the encounter and the body. The tribe had plenty of inquiries about the purported body. As the *Gazette* reports:

"Dexter Fallsdown, director of public safety for the Crow Tribe, described what he has heard: 'A Bigfoot got killed, some people came and picked him up and took him away.'"

Fallsdown refers to the conspiracy that government agents showed up, almost instantly, bagged the Bigfoot body up, and quickly left the scene.

Even the FBI's senior resident agent in Billings, Dan Vierthaler, was asked about the creature. He told the *Gazette*:

83

"That's the first I heard of it. I can assure you that we are not doing anything covertly to hide a body. I do not have a Bigfoot in my evidence locker."

The town of Plains, in Sanders County, was the site of an intriguing 2003 track find reported by the *Valley Press*. The tracks were found off River Road West on 87-year-old Jim Rohweder's property. Two other men, Dean Peterson, whose young son first spotted the tracks, and Bob Mesing, spent two hours following the track line into the woods. They lost the creature's trail when they reached an area with little snow and hard, rocky ground.

Messing reported that there were "hundreds and hundreds" of prints and he guessed by the tracks that the creature weighed between 800 and 1,000 pounds.

The path of the tracks indicated that the creature had emerged from the woods and walked toward Rohweder's shop where it triggered a motion light. Peterson, who lives next door to Rohweder, reported that at around 3:30 in the morning, he had been woken by his dog barking. Looking outside, about 45 yards from his window, he noticed the motion light on Rohweder's shop was on; however, there was nothing in view of the light and no indication of what had tripped it.

Peterson, a former police officer from Kalispell, and Mesing both agreed that the prints were not hoaxed, noting that it was clear from the prints that the creature's foot had an arch and was not flat-footed.

Mesing said the prints were like a human's but slightly squared, adding: "There were absolutely toes. It was absolutely not an animal that we would normally have seen out here...I have never seen anything like that."

According to Ray Crowe's *Bigfoot Behavior Volume II*, researcher Don Monroe interviewed a train engineer who spotted a Bigfoot walking alongside train tracks in August 2003 near Twin Meadows and Kalispell.

The engineer, Will Vasquez, said the BNSFR (Burlington Northern and Santa Fe Railway) train was heading north when it went around a corner through a rocky area along the river. The black, hairy creature was around eight feet tall. Due to the speed of the train, the sighting lasted only a few seconds.

On December 30, 2003, news broke that a Bigfoot had been shot by police officers in Montana. The term "news" should be used loosely here since the story's source turned out to be the tabloid *The Weekly World News*. As such stories sometimes do, rumors flew, and Montana state police found themselves having to answer calls regarding the purported dead Bigfoot.

Captain David Dill, head of the Billings regional office of the State Highway patrol, solemnly reported, "I can assure you; we didn't shoot a Bigfoot."

In March 2004, a woman and her daughter's boyfriend were on the highway above Clark Fork River on their way to St. Regis to pick up her daughter. It was a bright, Sunday afternoon and as they crossed the river, the woman spotted an unusual sight. As Lawrence and Ober recount in *Montana Myths and Legends*:

"I noticed the ice was breaking up from around the edges and floating downstream. As we started over the bridge that spans the river, I looked to my left, as I always do. There is a sand bar that reaches out into the river on the west side and near the tip I saw a very tall, eight to ten foot, hairy being and a much smaller one. It looked to be right at or just taller than the knee of the larger one."

The woman reported that the taller creature had long hair that was reddish brown in color.

The other passenger also spotted the creatures, but the pair continued their journey without stopping to observe any further. On the return trip later in the day, the creatures were nowhere to be seen.

The woman had the impression that she had observed a parent trying to teach its child something about the water, or perhaps just letting it carefully explore.

A veterinarian became a believer in the existence of Bigfoot after her sighting near Missoula in the summer of 2012.

The unnamed witness was hiking with her family on the Waterworks Trail around noon on July 20. They stopped for a quick break and observed a large, dark creature on the far ridge next to some power line poles. The creature stood completely still for 5-10 minutes. The witnesses stared at the figure, trying to comprehend what they were seeing. The creature suddenly turned, took several large steps, and vanished over the ridge.

The witness's daughter was able to capture a photo on an iPhone and the shot was posted on the BFRO website. The reporting witness told a BFRO representative that she "knows without a doubt she saw a Sasquatch."

While the photo unfortunately doesn't offer much in the way of evidence, the sighting is intriguing. A number of Bigfoot researchers have noted the frequency of sightings and accounts that involve the creatures being in close proximity to power lines, and this sighting falls in the same spectrum of such accounts.

On Labor Day weekend, 2004, a Bigfoot was spotted northeast of Helena, Lewis and Clark County, on the Missouri River. Ray Crowe reports the sighting in *Bigfoot Behavior Volume III*.

The witness was fly fishing on the river when a rock came zipping through the air and splashed into the water a few feet in front of him. Apparently, the man brushed the incident off, but a few moments later, another rock came. As he reports:

"I was thinking about changing my flies when dang if another rock didn't come flying out of nowhere splashing in front of me. Saw old Bigfoot in a squattin' position on the bank...it reached down and pulled up a big rock with one hand out of the river and heaved that sucker under hand at me. Man, here comes this rock at me with perfect aim!!!"

The witness managed to duck the rock just in time to see the creature grab another one to throw. The man wisely took the creature's hint and fled from the location.

In May 2006, a Democratic candidate for Flathead County commissioner made the news when it was pointed out that he had reported an encounter with Bigfoot.

Don Avery was a former administrator for the county

and had detailed his experience in a January 2005 blogpost. The post, now removed, recounted his sighting of a Bigfoot in Washington State in the early 2000s.

According to Browning's *Glacier Reporter*, Bigfoot activity was kicking up on the Blackfeet Reservation at the beginning of 2006. The March 2 edition of the paper ran a story about Bruch Schildt of Kiowa Camp. Schildt took his kids out on New Year's Day in 2006 and the group discovered tracks that measured eighteen inches long and ten inches wide. Schildt said the stride was about 39 inches. According to the newspaper:

"'I took my kids for an outing on New Year's Day,' said Bruce Schildt, who lives near Kiowa camp in Blackfeet country. 'I took them up Cut Bank Creek to play. We were on our way home, but we drove up toward the mountains by Grandpa's Lake. Toni Rae found a footprint, and we came back and took pictures and took them to Fish and Wildlife and they checked it out.'"

Schildt's kids had discovered a line of 30 to 40 large tracks in the snow. "The footprints looked like barefoot human footprints, but they were about three times as big," said Schildt, "They were frozen in the mud up there."

Gayle Skunkcap, director of Blackfeet Fish and Wildlife, investigated the scene and spoke with Glacier reporter John McGill:

"'I've never seen an official document as to whether Bigfoot exists or not,' he said, 'but I've also not seen an official document saying there's ever been any injury to anyone by a Bigfoot.'"

Of the tracks discovered by Schildt, Skunkcap said only one looked like it might come from something unusual, but his department is taking no chances. "People are calling and asking if I see one should I shoot it?" He said.

Skunkcap told the reporter that many of the calls were from concerned citizens asking if Bigfoot was living around their homes and asking what they should do about the creature.

Skunkcap stressed that shooting it was likely unnecessary

since there are no reports of the creatures attacking humans in the area.

"I'd say if you see one don't shoot because if it's someone playing a practical joke, you could wind up hurting somebody," Skunkcap stated. He further cautioned that the tracks could be human.

"There are a lot of trappers out with bear track snowshoes. There's a lot of pothole lakes up there, and trappers using bearpaws, but we take all calls seriously and we investigate."

Rumors about sightings continued to circulate in the area through the spring and into the summer. Bigfoot researchers from California and other regions journeyed to Montana to investigate but no further evidence was reported.

An anonymous report sent to Bobbie Short from a Montana man living in the Swan Mountains against the Flathead National Forest details his sighting of a possible Bigfoot. The report is dated September 6, 2007. In it, the witness recounts walking with his dog at dusk when he saw the silhouette of what appeared to be a person crouching behind a birch tree. The man called out a greeting, but the figure responded by quickly darting away.

"Whatever it was, I can tell you it was bipedal, fast, and very hairy. Probably around 6 feet tall or so."

Another report I was sent involved a boy out cutting wood with a chainsaw in 2009. Reportedly, the boy "sensed" something in the area and turned around to spot an eight-foot-tall creature. The boy said the beast looked like a silverback gorilla. The creature was standing upright, had a human-like face, and a "somewhat pointed head." The frightened boy ran away from the creature and reported the thing to his family.

There were other incidents around the home, too. The following month, the boy's father had a memorable experience. As the man reported:

"It was quite early in the morning and the sun was just coming over the mountain. I opened the back door and let the dogs do their morning business. About 50 feet from our back door was a large hairy man-like being. The dogs saw it as well and came running back into the house. I stood still on the stairs watching it. I think I was in shock by what I saw.

"The animal then turned and looked right at me and let out this scream/holler. It was the most frightening thing I have ever encountered. The yell struck every nerve in my body. I was so scared that it instantly made me cry."

The witness had a classic fight or flight response. Reportedly, he had never experienced such a level of fear in the woods. He was well familiar with Montana's wild animals, but he had never seen anything like the creature he witnessed standing before him. He described the beast:

"The animal was about 7-8 feet tall, and had brownish black hair covering its body. The hair was probably about 4-6 inches long. I would guess that it had to weigh 500+ pounds.

"When it let out that yell/scream at me, I got the feeling it was angry that I saw it. The face was like that of an ape but with very human features.

"I stood frozen to the stairs as it moved off down the hill. The experience probably lasted only a couple of minutes. It walked on two legs and was no bear!"

The man was adamant that the creature he saw was not a bear, having been face to face with some of the state's large animals including bear, elk, and mountain lion. He is confident that what he saw was something completely different. He reiterated the disturbing experience he had when the creature screamed: "When it let out that yell/scream was what really touched a fear in me."

At the September 2011 meeting of the Western Bigfoot Society, Don Monroe spoke about the potential high intelligence of Bigfoot, specifically, the theory that the creatures sometimes braid the hair of horses.

Monroe related an account from an equestrian woman in Montana who claimed that younger Bigfoots, who had smaller fingers, were responsible for the braids that appear on horses' manes.

According to the group's meeting minutes, the report stated that braids "range from simple three strands to more complicated ones similar to a French braid and are tied off with a tight hair knot."

While there are occasional reports of horses turning up with their manes mysteriously braided, the idea that Bigfoot is the culprit is, at the least, controversial.

More Bigfoot news came out of Montana in August 2012, but this time the story was a tragic one and was reported by numerous state news agencies.

On Sunday, August 26, a forty-four-year-old man named Randy Lee Tenley decided to try his hand at some hoaxing. Tenley's plan went awry, and he was struck by two vehicles and killed just south of Kalispell.

Tenley had donned a ghillie suit, a type of full body camouflage outfit used by military snipers, and was standing in the right-hand lane of U.S. Highway 93 when he was struck by the first car. The second one struck him as he lay in the road. The drivers were both teenaged girls, 15 and 17 years of age.

After interviews with some of Tenley's friends, state trooper Jim Schneider verified the man's motives. Officer Schneider told reporters:

"He was trying to make people think he was Sasquatch so people would call in a Sasquatch sighting. You can't make it up. I haven't seen or heard of anything like this before. Obviously, his suit made it difficult for people to see him."

A man driving between WSS and Checkerboard, west of Sutherland Lake on December 2, 2012, spotted a Bigfoot along the road moving at a quick pace. As the witness reports:

"It was about 250 to 300 yards away and I could make it out quite well. The thing was on two legs, had very long arms that seemed to end barely above the knees. Its head was positioned as if a person were sticking their neck out, and it ran while barely moving its arms. It didn't look like it was alarmed, just as if it were just going along its way heading back into the mountains. In scale to the trees, I'd say it was about six and a half feet tall."

The BFRO report on the incident doesn't offer any details on the creature's coloring or features.

Joshua Cutchin and Timothy Renner mention an odd Montana incident in the second volume of *Where the Footprints End*. The report comes from Brian "Duke" Sullivan, a Bigfoot investigator and podcast host who had the experience in 2015.

Sullivan spotted what he first thought was a tree stump with a pattern resembling a face. He intended to film the stump with his video camera as an example of pareidolia but then noticed that the expression on the "stump" changed.

Now realizing that he was witnessing a Sasquatch, the man elected to leave the area rather than disturb it.

The *Great Falls Tribune* ran an article in its April 1, 2019, issue discussing Bigfoot sightings. Apparently, the paper thought it would be funny to feature reports of the creature in its April Fool's edition. Perhaps they were taking a swipe at people who take the topic seriously. Whatever the case, the paper did report on some actual accounts of Sasquatch sightings, starting off with an account from a truck driver named "J.G."

The man reports that he saw one of the creatures along a lonely stretch of Decker Highway at midnight in October 2006. At first, he thought he was seeing a hitchhiker, at least, until it started crossing the road in front of him. As the paper reports:

"He slammed on the brakes. The creature was at least 8 feet tall and had 8-to 10-inch-long hair, 'almost like it was groomed.'"

Reportedly, the driver returned to the scene the following day and measured bushes, fences, and other objects in the area to try to confirm the creature's size. Unfortunately, he found no tracks or other evidence that the Bigfoot had been in the area.

A man out on a wrecker call in Philips County in January 2011 saw a creature on Highway 191 in the C.M. Russell Wildlife Refuge. It was about 1 a.m. when the driver reached the location a mile north of the Missouri River. As he reports to the BFRO:

"I was loading a car onto my truck when I heard a deep

grunt. I turned with my flashlight and looked behind me and almost 100 feet behind me was an upright walking creature dragging the dead elk that the car I was towing had hit down the side of a hill. It was about 40 below zero. I was cold and scared, so I loaded up and got back to town."

In a follow-up interview, the witness clarified that there was a full moon on the night of his sighting that aided his view of the Sasquatch. He said the creature was between 7 ½ to 8 feet in height with brown, graying hair. The shoulders were broad, and the beast had long arms and a big, square, flat face. It used only one hand to drag the elk away by the antlers.

The witness shined a light on the creature and the thing's eyes reflected like those of a deer caught in headlights. It looked at the man briefly, then continued dragging the elk away.

Kalispell's paper, the *Daily Inter Lake*, reported in its September 10, 2017, edition on Misty Allabaugh, who reported she had been tracking Sasquatch in Montana for 24 years. The Columbia Falls resident saw a Sasquatch when she was seventeen years old in 1993. She was with her parents at the time, but the elder Allabaughs didn't make a big deal of the sighting.

Misty's mother gasped and asked her daughter if she had seen the hairy man crossing the road, while her father simply told her to just let it go. But Mary couldn't let it go. As the paper reports:

"Her father had worked backcountry logging jobs all his life and had seen some odd occurrences through the years that couldn't easily be explained. He'd been told if you leave "it" alone, it will leave you alone.

"Then Allabaugh saw it with her own eyes. It was like nothing she'd ever seen before, but she knew it was Bigfoot. 'There's no doubt in my mind,' she said. 'It was on a short hill. You could see the daylight between his arms, his hair lifting in the breeze.'"

Allabaugh continued to research the topic of Bigfoot as she grew older. While she has traveled to other regions to do field research, her main focus has been Montana, specifically, the area between Kalispell and Libby.

Allabaugh says she has evidence she has collected over the years, including hair, blood, and excrement samples, but she doesn't have the resources to have testing done. Still, she presses on and tries to take a scientific approach. Allabaugh told the *Inter Lake*, "If it's what we think, it's something between prehistoric and a mountain gorilla."

NBC news in Montana reported on the search for Bigfoot in the state on November 1, 2019. The news spoke with Joe Hauser, owner of the Montana Vortex and House of Mystery outside Glacier National Park. Hauser told reporters that he certainly believes in Bigfoot. As the story related:

"Hauser walks the grounds every day. He bought the property to study the electromagnetic anomaly. He's the first to tell you weird things happen there.

"'A lot of people come in totally skeptical, and then they leave and go. I don't know what's going on here, but there's definitely something going on here,' Hauser said."

At the attraction, Hauser displays casts of Sasquatch footprints collected from various locations. He says his interest was sparked when he first saw the famous Patterson Gimlin film of a Bigfoot in Northern California.

Hauser heard some weird screams in 1983 that he believes were Bigfoot, but twenty-two years later, he had a sighting; this time, he was at Avalanche Lake in Glacier Park with his son. He recalls the incident:

"He looks across the lake and goes, 'Hey Dad, there's two Bigfoot walking across that snow field there.' And sure enough—big strides, great big arm swings, arms down to their knees. And we had about a 5-minute sighting walking across the snow field."

Hauser told the news that the creatures will knock on his house at night and that they leave signs around the property.

He's seen the creatures as recently as the fall of 2018 on a trail at the vortex. Tourists have also reported Bigfoot in the area.

"We have lots of sightings here; they're just not reported," Hauser said. "We take reports in here almost every week. And this is all over Montana—Georgetown Lake, Anaconda—and people have been having experiences down there for years. Glacier Park has a lot of sightings up there."

The BFRO received a report from a witness who was riding a snowmobile in Jefferson County on March 9, 2019. The witness posted the following description:

"I was up snowmobiling in the Elk Horns, and I saw a very tall creature about 200 yards away. I'd say the shoulders had to be 5 feet wide and it was probably 9 feet tall. I watched it for a minute, then I got freaked out and left. The sighting occurred around twelve noon and two other witnesses were present.

In a follow up on the report, investigators learned that the creature had "very dark charcoal, or deep gray to black hair." The witness did not see any facial features but noticed large biceps.

After about a minute of observation, the witness and his friends left the scene. When they passed by the spot again several hours later, the creature was gone.

On June 12, 2019, at 12:35 p.m., a motorist driving up Crane Mountain road in Flathead County saw a large, black creature run up the side of a mountain. The witness first thought it was a bear and pulled off to get a better look. According to the BFRO report:

"I looked up to see a bipedal creature or whatever it was taking large strides up the steep incline up the hill. After 70 yards it stopped and looked at me, then continued up the mountain out of sight. It was completely covered in jet black hair, and when the sun hit its hair, it shined a brass or copper color."

When BFRO investigators Caitlin and Thomas Ertz followed up with the witness, they learned that he had returned to the location the following day and attempted to make a cast of tracks found in the area. The follow up report on the BFRO website notes:

"Cast was not recoverable, as it broke into many pieces

when attempting to retrieve. He only was able to cast one track. He brought his girlfriend up and there appeared to be two sets of tracks, one slightly bigger than his 12-boot size, and another quite a bit larger. He did not have a measurement of either."

The witness took the Ertzes to the exact location of his sighting and the investigators noticed an abundance of edible plants in the area, including wild strawberries, blackberries, huckleberries, morel mushrooms, and more. A nearby creek is a source of fresh water.

The witness stressed to the investigators how impressed he was with the creature's easy movement, noting that it took the thing less than ten seconds to climb the steep embankment.

The witness was extremely uncomfortable being back at the location of his sighting.

A truck driver traveling in Mineral County on Interstate 90 near Lookout Pass in the Bitterroot Range saw a Bigfoot standing on the back side of a concrete barrier. It was 4:30 a.m. in April 2020 when the incident occurred.

The sighting lasted only 5 to 10 seconds, but the creature was illuminated by the truck's high beams. The creature's hair was long and reddish-brown in color. According to the witness, an avid hunter and outdoorsman, the Bigfoot moved extremely fast and was quickly out of sight. The witness reported his sighting to the BFRO in June 2020.

PART THREE
Water Monsters

Legends of Lakes and Rivers

With plenty of fresh water in Montana, it's not surprising that the state has some interesting monster legends associated with some of the bodies of water.

Tribal lore from several Native Nations mentioned curious legends of unknown water creatures.

The longest river in North America, the Missouri River, flows through Montana and is reportedly the home of a water monster, said by Native Americans to be a horned serpent.

Ronald Haller was floating downriver near Fort Benton in Chouteau County in the summer of 1970 when a 6-8-foot-long black fish struck his boat with so much force that it dented the fiberglass hull. The incident was reported in the January 27, 1971, edition of the *Missoulan*.

Reportedly, Haller caught footage of the fish with the movie camera he had at hand, but the film has never, umm, surfaced.

In the classic *Mysterious America*, author Loren Coleman lists creatures known as "Ooogle-Boogles" that reportedly live in Waterton Lake in the Waterton Lakes National Park. While the greater portion of the park and its lake is in Canada, the southern tip is in Glacier County, Montana.

Locals on both the United States and Canadian sides of the water mention the existence of the aquatic beasts. The creatures are said to have long necks, cow-like heads, and humped backs that are visible above the surface when the creatures move about. Multiple accounts refer to "baby monsters" of the same description living in the lake.

It's possible that the creatures are of the same species that cryptozoologist Ivan Sanderson mentions in his book *Things*. Sanderson reports that in 1922, a man who owned a summer cottage on the lake reportedly saw a strange creature, 35-40 feet in length with two horns, or perhaps tentacles, on its head. The man said the creature swam with an undulating motion as it moved through the lake.

Water Babies

According to the Crow people, strange animals and spirits have lived in the region's waters since ancient times. According to the Crow, the creatures are always hungry and are a danger to humans.

The Tongue River in southeastern Montana and the Little Bighorn River in Big Horn County were said to be the homes of monsters that had human form, albeit a somewhat distorted human form. They were said to be very fat, with arms and legs of unusual size and were purportedly so horrible looking that most people would flee at the sight of them.

Reportedly, there were creatures said to be in a lake at the head of the Little Bighorn River that resembled children. Some thought they were spirits, but the implication was that they were dangerous creatures taking a human form.

Curiously, this harkens to the water baby legends that I have explored in other locations, particularly, Pyramid Lake in Nevada where the Paiute tribe say the creatures have long lived.

The neighboring Shoshone Nation also has stories of creepy water baby type creatures that they call "pah-o-nah."

One location in Montana associated with the little creatures is a hot spring in the Bitterroot Valley that has been known as both Weeping Child Hot Springs and Sleeping Child Hot Springs.

There are various tales that explain how the site got its name. The most mundane but tragic account involves the death of a Native American child who was lost in the water before the child's mother could save it.

Another account claims that an early settler in the area

found a crying child lying on the ground near the water and gave the spot its name.

But the most fascinating, and weird accounts, are the stories that say the water was named because of strange creatures that made it home, creatures that preyed on human victims. Stories from early Bitterroot pioneers recount the stories told by Salish natives who were familiar with the hot springs.

The creepy legend says that travelers who passed through the area would hear the sorrowful crying of a child. Searching for the source of the crying, the traveler would soon discover a child left alone on the banks of the water. Those who found the child would assume it was abandoned and starving. Attempting to calm the baby, the traveler would stick a finger in its mouth as a pacifier. The child would immediately stop crying and suck at the finger, but while doing so, it would mesmerize its rescuer.

The child would suck at the finger so hard that it pulled the flesh off the finger and continued up the hand, and arm, and on and on until it had devoured all the flesh off the poor good Samaritan's body.

The dry, bare bones would fall to the ground in a pile and the "child" would resume its position on the ground, waiting for the next unsuspecting victim to pass by.

Whatever it was, the dreadful creature was never satisfied and was always hungry. Reportedly, there was a great pile of bones in the area from all the creature's victims.

Later settlers renamed the creek and springs Sleeping Child. The area was bought from natives in the 1800s and a resort was opened to take advantage of the healing hot springs. Over the years, the area has changed hands numerous times. Today, there's a luxurious lodge/retreat at the site.

Olin D. Wheeler's *The Trail of Lewis and Clark* mentions the weird story of the weeping child and it was covered in later years by Ruth Thorning in *What's in a Bitterroot Place* Name published by the *Bitterroot Star.*

The Flathead River and Flathead Lake

The Kalispel tribe has a tale about a monster that lived in Flathead Lake during the tribe's early days in the area. Legend says that while a hunting party was camped by the lake, a monster rose out of the water's depths and headed for the men. The hunters quickly picked up their bows and started firing arrows at the massive creature, hoping to bring it down before it reached them.

The stream of arrows proved useless, they simply bounced off the creature's thick skin. With their weapons ineffective, the hunters raced from the scene, hoping to get away from the beast. One man was defiant and stood his ground, continuing to fire arrows at the thing. His bravery proved his undoing. The creature seized the man in its large mouth and dragged him to the water where it plunged back into the lake with its victim.

After the event, the Flatheads purportedly avoided the lake and did their fishing elsewhere.

Traditional native legends say that the Flathead River, which flows southward from Flathead Lake, was created due to the activity of a giant beaver that used to live in the region.

According to oral tradition, the giant beaver lived in the lake long before native people arrived in the area and it was a massive creature. Joseph H. Wherry mentions the giant beaver in *Indian Masks & Myths of the West*:

"In the lake, just south of the city of Kalispell, lived Giant Beaver, who was so immense that even a dozen warriors could not conquer him. It is said that he lived when a river flowed out of the west side of the lake many thousands of years ago. It was then that Giant Beaver constructed a dam across the opening in the lake because he was getting so large that the lake was too shallow for him. Ancient Flathead River dried up and the lake got deeper and deeper, and to keep all of his water, Beaver built another dam across the south end of the lake and he was happy."

According to the lore, an especially long, hard winter struck, causing much more snow to accumulate than normal. The snow piled deep on the frozen lake and when the end of winter came, a warm Chinook wind roared through the valley of the Giant Beaver, bringing an unseasonably warm night. The snow quickly melted, coming down the mountainside in avalanches. As large as the beaver was, and as strong as his dam was, the sudden rush was too much for the dam to hold and when it broke, it flowed out on the south side of the lake, creating the Flathead River.

Wherry reports that the giant beaver story has associations with multiple native tribes in the region, including the Flathead, Kootenai, Nez Perce, and Blackfoot.

Reportedly, the creation of the river also brought mountain bison to the area and bison still roam the region today. About thirty miles south of Flathead Lake is the National Bison Range near Dixon and Ravalli.

Legend says a giant beaver once called Montana home.

The stories do not say what became of the giant beaver, and while some may brush the tale off as mythology, it's not one that should be dismissed too soon. During the Pleistocene epoch, colloquially referred to as the Ice Age, a giant beaver was indeed alive and well in North America. Scientists say the species *Castoroides* was a beaver the size of a bear that could grow as large as 7.2 feet in length. Fossils of the creature were first discovered in a peat bog in Ohio in 1837. Scientists later determined that the animal could once be found throughout the continental United States and Canada.

Castoroides went extinct during the Pleistocene–Holocene Transition 12,800–11,500 years ago.

Are the native legends from Montana a cultural memory of this massive, ancient beaver? Whatever the case, the proven, historical existence of the giant beaver adds a different perspective to the native legends of the river's creation.

The waters of Flathead Lake and the Flathead River both seem to be a magnet for monstrous legends. Another native tale associated with the lake comes from the Kootenai tradition and was told in 1955 by Madeline Lefthand and interpreted by Adeline Matthias.

This story has been published in multiple sources, including Clark's *Indian Legends of the Northern Rockies*, though I relate the tale here as I learned it via conversation with a Montana associate.

According to the legend, a band of natives lived on an island in Flathead Lake not far from Elmo. One winter, they decided to strike their camp and move. Since the lake was frozen, the band set off across the ice.

Halfway across the lake, two girls came upon a two-foot-long antler sticking up out of the ice. One girl decided she was going to chop the antler off and keep it, but her companion cautioned her against doing so.

The first girl was determined and told her friend that she realized the danger but had special power to escape if anything happened. As it turned out, both the girls had a "special power." One could transform into a ball, and the other into a buckskin target, and both were certain they could reach land if anything happened to them on the ice.

The girls waited until most of the other people were almost on shore, then the first girl started cutting the antler. When she had cut through to the middle of the antler, it started to shake. The ice started breaking up and the head of a monster appeared, shaking its antlers.

The girls used their powers to reach the safety of shore, but due to the violent breaking of the ice, half of their band had fallen in the freezing lake and drowned.

Lefthand says the loss of life during the event explains why there are so few Kootenai.

"The monster was never seen again, but our people never again went out very far on the lake. Not many years ago, some white men who were fishing on Flathead Lake said that they had seen a strange animal in the water."

Lefthand is clearly referring to a sighting of the Flathead Lake monster (discussed in depth elsewhere in this volume).

This particular water monster story isn't unique to the Kootenai. A similar tale is told by both the Blackfeet and

Sarcees, though the legend is connected to a Canadian lake in those cases. A similar account can also be found among a band of Nez Perce around the Snake River.

Reportedly, in 1915, a school of sturgeon was spotted near Plains in the Clark Fork River sixty miles downstream from Flathead Lake. The fish were reported to be heading toward the lake though there is continued controversy over whether there are actually sturgeon in the Flathead.

The May 27, 1937, edition of the *Flathead Courier* reported that a man fishing from a bridge over the Flathead River got a bird's eye view of something monstrous swimming by. At first glance, the witness thought it was a dog in the water but looking closer, he realized the creature was at least six feet in length.

The man was an experienced outdoorsman and looking closely, he realized it was not anything he was familiar with, ruling out beavers, otters, bears and other known creatures.

As it swam by, the thing held its head out of the water. According to the fisherman, the beast had a long mane of brown hair on its neck.

Lair of the Flathead Lake Monster.

Flathead Lake Monster

Flathead Lake is the largest natural freshwater lake west of the Mississippi in the contiguous 48 states. The lake is 28 miles long and 15 miles wide with 185 miles of shoreline.

The lake sits in the northwest corner of Montana about seven miles south of Kalispell. It's the remnant of an ancient, massive glacial lake and is home to a range of aquatic species, including bull trout, cutthroat trout, mountain whitefish, and more. Over the years many non-native species have been introduced to the lake, including rainbow trout, northern pike, and kokanee salmon.

The lake is a sportsman's paradise and a popular spot for boating and other water-based activities. Each year, tourists flock to the area and enjoy its natural beauty and recreational opportunities.

The picturesque lake may also be home to a water monster.

According to native traditions, monsters have been in Flathead Lake for a very long time and tribal oral traditions have many stories related to monstrous fish and other strange aquatic creatures.

Descriptions of the Flathead Lake monster vary with some reporting it as a giant fish, while others point to something more prehistoric in appearance. Locals have dubbed the beast "Flessie" in a nod to the more famous Nessie, Scotland's Loch Ness monster.

The first widely reported sighting came from Captain James Kern, of the steamboat *US Grant*, who spotted the monster in 1889. Kern saw what he first thought was another boat heading toward him, but as it grew closer, he realized it was a large animal, similar to a whale. One of the steamboat's passengers fired at the creature with a rifle, causing it to submerge to safety.

In 1899, Joe Zelezny was spearfishing by torchlight with some friends north of what is today the town of Rollins. In an oral interview, Zelezny reported that he and his friends often fished at night to gather food for their families. They were in a shallow bay and had finished for the evening when Joe's friends told him they had seen something unusual lying in the lake on the bottom of the shallows. They described it as ten to twelve feet in length and log shaped. Intrigued, Joe handed his brother Henry a spear and told him to go and stick the object.

When Henry stuck the object, it shot up out of the water. According to Zelezny:

"I think it was a sturgeon. That's what I think it was. I couldn't describe another fish like it, but still it didn't' look exactly like a sturgeon, either, but it couldn't have been anything else."

Ellen Baumler, who relates the tale in her book *Beyond Spirit Tailings*, reports that Zelezny was considered an honest homesteader with no interest in promoting the idea of the Flathead monster.

In 1919, another steamboat captain saw something odd in the water. At first, he thought it was a log and took action to avoid the object. Once he changed course, the "log" came to life and swam around his vessel on the starboard side. It was seen by 50 passengers on the ship.

In the 1920s, commercial salmon trawling was started on the lake. Reportedly, during this time, there were frequent reports from fishermen that their nets, which were designed to catch forty-pound fish, would sometimes come up shredded, as if something massive had torn through.

Ila Rose Wilcox Chappel of Bigfork waited a long time to tell her Flathead monster story. She wrote to the *Flathead Courier* in 1965 to recall an incident from 40 years prior.

Chappel reported that sometime between 1922 and 1923, her family, along with two others, were moving to the east side of the lake from Denton, Montana. They shipped their household goods by rail to the town of Somers where the items were ferried across by boat and barge.

Sadly, there was an accident near the middle of the lake and a barge full of their belongings filled with water and sank. Chappel reports that everything was lost. She told the paper:

"For weeks and months, we searched for floating objects in the water and on shore. One time, as my brother was riding in the boat and looking into the water, it seemed he saw a great big log following the boat. Finally, it came up alongside and seemed to be passing. When my brother said, 'Look!' it flipped its tail and was gone. It was about 15 feet long."

Over the years, various attempts have been made to capture the famous monster. In July 1964, one fisherman tried baiting hooks with whole chickens and lumps of liver, but he came up empty handed.

Skin diver Fuller Laugher of Malta spent four days systematically searching for the monster, but he also came up with no results.

Some believe the Flathead monster is a giant sturgeon.

Skeptics have suggested a range of animals as the culprits for the monster sightings, including beavers, otters, and other known animals, but such creatures simply would not explain the wide range of accounts.

The most likely culprit, if indeed the monster is a real, known animal, is the giant sturgeon. Sturgeon are prehistoric looking fish and can reach massive proportions. Many people who have seen the Flathead Lake monster affirm that it is indeed a sturgeon. The problem is sturgeon are not really caught in

Flathead Lake. There is, however, a historic exception to this.

In the 1950s, a company named Big Fish Unlimited saw the monster legend as an opportunity to attract attention and boost tourism for the lake. They offered a cash reward for the capture of Flathead Lake's mysterious creature.

Sure enough, someone came in to collect the bounty. C. Leslie Griffith presented a 7 ½ foot long white sturgeon that weighed in at just over 181 pounds. Griffith said he had hooked the sturgeon off Cromwell Island on the night of May 28, 1955. According to the fisherman, it took him five hours to reel the beast in.

Some proclaimed that the Flathead monster had finally been caught, but others were doubtful. Skeptics of the catch believed the sturgeon had been trucked in from elsewhere so it could be "caught" in Flathead Lake, a ploy, they believed, to collect the offered reward. It wasn't just the size of the catch, it was the fact that no sturgeon had been caught in the lake at all, ever.

Not only was there debate over the location that the sturgeon had been caught, but a legal battle over it ensued. Griffith swore in court that the fish had indeed been hooked in Flathead Lake.

Polson journalist Paul Fugleberg reported that the case went all the way to the Montana Supreme Court, but still, the story is, at best, murky and the case was about more than just the validity of the sturgeon's presence in Flathead Lake. Griffith and Big Fish Unlimited were at odds over the display of the fish.

A District Court finally ruled that Big Fish Unlimited owned the sturgeon since Griffith had turned it in for the reward. But the court also ruled that Griffith was entitled to a share of the proceeds from the display of the fish.

So, was Griffith's sturgeon really caught in Flathead Lake or is it just a fish story? According to Laney Hanzel, a biologist from Missoula looked at the contents of the sturgeon's stomach and found that it contained organisms not found in Flathead Lake. So, while some believe the sturgeon is the legendary monster, others have serious doubts. Whatever the case, Griffith's catch is now on display at the Polson Flathead Historic Museum.

Laney Hanzel and Paul Fugleberg, both mentioned above,

are significant in the history of the lake's legend.

Fugleberg was a local writer and was editor of Polson's *Flathead Courier*. He collected accounts of the lake monster and wrote numerous articles about the creature, reporting on sightings when they popped up.

Laney Hanzel, a retired fisheries biologist with Montana Fish, Wildlife and Parks, has long kept track of monster sightings from the lake. Hanzel notes that sightings of the monster are essentially divided into two groups.

"The object most frequently (seventy percent) described is a large eel-shape creature that reaches in length from twenty to forty feet. It is round, brown to blue-black in color, and possesses very obvious steel-black eyes and undulating hips. Others identify it as a large-sized fish from six to ten feet in length."

Hanzel hasn't seen the creature himself, but he does report that on more than one occasion, he pulled in fishing nets only to discover massive holes made by something too large to be explained by the lake's known fauna.

Noting the number of people who have reported the monster, Hanzel says:

"Details of the creature have been described by mothers, doctors, lawyers, biologists, engineers, anglers, and policemen. The sighters were not drinking or on drugs and they hate to talk about it to anyone for fear of being identified as a 'weirdo' or worse."

Fugleberg notes that while he was editor of the *Courier,* he was given some words of wisdom from then secretary of the Montana Press Association, Dorothy M. Johnson:

"I don't think the monster should be done with tongue in cheek. You have eyewitness accounts by people who were scared and didn't think it was funny. I remember hearing about *something* in Flathead Lake more than forty years ago, so don't give the Polson Chamber of Commerce credit for dreaming it up."

Sightings

Over the decades there have been many sightings of the Flathead Lake monster. Here are some of the highlights and significant sightings of the creature. It's notable that some witnesses are adamant that what they saw was a giant fish, while others believe they spotted something more unusual and unknown.

In the late 1940s, Joe Krall of Sunburst saw something massive in the water. Krall's account was detailed in an article in *Montana Outdoors* (November-December 1991 issue).

Krall wrote a letter to wildlife officials and reported that he and some friends had been camping on Cromwell Island and took a boat trip around Wild Horse Island. They coasted into a cove, with a 40-50 feet diameter, and watched some deer on a nearby slope. A half dozen large fish were active in the water around their boat, swam under it, then quickly went out into deep water. Krall said the fish were about five feet in length and possibly over 100 pounds each. He recalls:

"Our eyesight was clear, the sun was right, the bottom was visible about six feet below us, and the water was clear. They were fish, not monsters; I assumed they were sturgeon. If not, what were they?"

On Sunday, July 10, 1949, the H.W. (Buck) Black family were at Chatwood's Narrows Resort about six miles north of Polson. The Black family included Buck and his wife Mary, and their children, ten-year-old Judy, Laird, 7, Fred, 5, and a family friend, seven-year-old Mark Rolfson.

The Blacks were in a fourteen-foot boat with an outboard motor, and they were on a mission. They were headed out to tow back another small boat. They reached the second boat, connected a tow line, and started the return trip at about 3:30 in the afternoon.

Young Judy was riding in the towed boat as the family headed to Polson. Buck started tinkering with the motor but snapped to attention when his wife suddenly screamed.

The family had barely left the Narrows and Buck's first thought was that someone had fallen overboard. Mary was pointing east, her eyes wide and her mouth open in shock. Following the direction Mary was pointing, Buck saw something in the water, but it wasn't what he expected. About 150 feet away was a large fish. It was swimming on the surface, and as he watched, it made an abrupt turn. Approximately six feet of its back was visible, but the thing's head was submerged.

The boaters watched the creature for about thirty seconds. Black later stated: "The fish swam in a southeasterly direction, rolling out a wake six to eight inches high as it gradually submerged."

A reporter with the local *Flathead Courier* listened to the family's story. Mary and Buck differed on one point. Mary had recalled seeing a dorsal fin on the creature, but Buck did not. Buck, however, was positive he knew what the family had seen: "I am convinced the monster is a huge sturgeon and is at least 10 to 12 feet long."

Buck Black's sighting carries some additional weight when his background is considered—he was a former member and chairman of the Montana Fish and Game Commission. Years later, he stood by his original conviction that the Flathead monster, at least the one that he spotted, was a large sturgeon.

Janet and Colin Bord's *Alien Animals* reports on a family's sighting of the creature in 1960. On a Friday in September, the Zigler family were out at the lakeside at the Polson Country Club when they heard a disruption in the water and decided to investigate. They walked to a nearby pier where they observed a creature rubbing itself against the pilings. They noted the action was akin to the way a cow would rub itself against a gatepost.

Mr. Zigler went to retrieve his rifle. Mrs. Zigler continued to watch the creature and saw it raise its head up out of the water. She reported: "It was a horrible looking thing, with a head about the size of a horse and about a foot of neck showing."

Mrs. Zigler screamed at the sight of the beast and her husband got back just in time to see the creature swimming away at a "great rate of speed."

Mr. Zigler said he was familiar with sturgeon and was certain that what he had observed was not a sturgeon of any kind. The Ziglers had another sighting of the same creature the following week.

Ronald Nixon and his brother Maynard thought that the Flathead creature was a joke. In fact, the two men had hoaxed photos of the water monster, but their attitude changed on September 21, 1962. The two men were driving along the Polson waterfront when they saw something strange in the lake. They stopped the car and stared in disbelief before confirming with each other that they had seen the same thing. The March 31, 1963, edition of the *Great Falls Tribune* recalled Nixon's statement:

"We had a good view looking down on the water from only about 300 feet away. It was moving straight away from shore and fast enough so the wave at the front was about two feet high. The wake at the back must have been at least 25 feet from the front, so the object must have been longer than that. There was no fin on the back. It couldn't have been a sturgeon. I don't have any idea what it was."

Montana writer Paul Fugleberg, who recorded sightings of the monster, recorded a September 8, 1963, sighting of the creature witnessed by Polson high school teachers Heather McLeod and Genevieve Parratt. The pair was boating around 11:30 in the morning when they spotted what they described as a ten-foot-long gray creature swimming rapidly through the water. Three humps were visible, and the thing left a three-foot wake behind as it passed by.

A posting on the website Cryptozoo-oscity details an encounter from the summer of 1964.

Joyce Nelson and her family were swimming offshore at Polson when they had a close encounter with an unseen aquatic creature. She reports that several swimmers felt something large brush against their legs.

"After much screaming and fuss, we all got up on the dock. We were watching and a large creature similar to, but not quite, a sturgeon was seen about one hundred feet from us."

Paul Fugleberg's booklet, *Montana Nessie of Flathead Lake*, contains an incident from August 1, 1965. A man named Earl House, and his son Richard, of Claremont, CA, were checking into the Queens Court Motel in Polson when desk clerk Myrtle Koehler saw something strange in the lake's waters. The object was moving past one of the orange buoys in the lake and it dipped up and down as it moved. The trio watched from the motel as the thing moved westward on a parallel to the shoreline.

A young woman who was in the area rushed into the office in excitement, shouting "look, a submarine."

Koehler looked through a pair of binoculars and reported that she thought the thing had a silvery dorsal fin.

Curiously, as the creature moved through the water, it passed a teenage girl who was swimming near the old Polson Lumber Company's mill site. The girl didn't notice the creature but did experience the wake it created. She later stated that she thought the wake was due to a boat, but none of the observers had seen any boats in the vicinity at the time.

Fugleberg also collected an account from a family who spotted the creature later the same month, and again, the idea of a submarine was proposed by one of the witnesses.

On August 19, 1965, the Funke family was having dinner on the patio of their home on the lake's west shore overlooking Indian Bay, when Mrs. Funke saw something swimming toward the family's dock. The creature was creating a large wake, and according to the couple's son, Robert, it resembled a surfacing submarine.

Robert Funke was a Major in the US military and was home on leave from Viet Nam. He ran into the house to retrieve a movie camera, but by the time he got back outside, the thing had vanished.

The Funkes described the creature as shiny black in color with a large fin on its back. They said that it seemed to roll over as it swam.

Two younger members of the family, Bobby, 13, and Larry, 12, were out in a boat when the creature passed by. They didn't spot it themselves but reported that their boat had been rocked by a big wave that seemed to come from beneath the surface of the water.

On June 5, 1970, Neil DeGolier Sr. of Polson, and his son, Neil Jr., along with Don Johnson of Anacortes, WA, saw a weird creature in the water. DeGolier senior told a reporter with the *Flathead Courier* that the thing was "lizard colored" and that it looked like it had the head of an African rhino minus the snout and ears. DeGolier estimated that the creature was ten feet in length.

According to the Nov-Dec 1991 issue of *Montana Outdoors*, a group of people in a motorboat chased the monster in 1971. Lori Evelend of Rocker was out with three friends on a late Sunday afternoon in June. The group pulled out of West Shore State Park in a fourteen-foot motorboat to do some fishing around Yellow Bay. Evelend details the incident:

"We weren't very far from Yellow Bay, about a half-mile, when on our right about 100 feet away this creature appeared. Jack turned the boat toward it as we all looked at each other with the thought, 'I didn't see that if you didn't see that.' I also thought, 'My God, this is like a dog chasing a car. What is Jack going to do when he catches it?'"

But the boaters never caught the monster. When they were within 75 feet, the creature dove out of sight, then reappeared at another spot on the left side of the boat. The man at the wheel turned the boat trying to keep up with the creature, but it dove again and vanished for good.

The witness said that while it was in view, three humps were visible about five feet above the water. The creature was estimated to be about thirty feet long.

Paul Fugleberg reported an August 26, 1974, sighting. Larry and Nona Mahugh of Polson were out with a friend, a

Thai college student named Chi, for some fishing off Angel Point on the lake's west shore. It was about 8:30 in the morning and the trio saw an unusual sight; a large fish swam as close as 30 feet from the shore at an amazing speed. Chi estimated the creature was about 12 feet in length.

On July 31, 1982, at about 5:30 in the evening, Mrs. Alva Olsen and her sister Gladys Owen of Seeley Lake were enjoying themselves at the Olsen home on the west shore of the lake four miles from Polson.

According to the account, collected by Paul Fugleberg, the ladies were surprised to see the calm water disrupted by a large creature 100 yards offshore. The witnesses reported that the thing was around 20 feet in length and dark brown or black in color. Two humps were visible as the creature moved at a brisk pace. Mrs. Olsen reported that the monster's head was "oval shaped and larger than a football."

The Olsens reported that several years prior, a family friend had a weird experience on the lake. The friend, a 23-year-old college student from Indiana, was sailing in the Olsen's boat in front of the home but ended her outing abruptly. She docked the boat and entered the house, pale and shaken, from something she had seen on the lake. She later told the Olsens that while sailing, a long, brown snake-like creature had come alongside the craft and swam underneath. She returned immediately, clearly not wanting to have any further encounter with whatever it was.

Don Knight of Missoula spotted a monster fish in the lake on August 20, 1983. He and five others were enjoying a day boating when they spotted the creature:

"When we got about 30 yards from it, it started moving and came out of the water. Then you could see it perfectly. I'm not exaggerating. We couldn't believe what we were seeing. That was the biggest freshwater fish I've ever seen. It was 25-30 feet long. Its fin was about two feet out of the water, and it was cutting the water like a shark."

Knight told an AP (Associated Press) reporter that when the creature passed the bow it "sent a wave off that would put my fifteen-foot boat to shame."

The group observed the fish for about four minutes as it swam close and in front of the boat. Knight reported seeing ridges, humps, and scales, confirming his notion that it was likely a sturgeon.

Another sighting reported from the summer of 1985 comes from a registered nurse. The witness posted his account on Monsterwatch Project, a "not quite official" site for Flathead monster reports. The site removes witness names, but reportedly keeps them on file.

The 1985 incident occurred between 7:30-8:00 a.m. on a sunny day. The reporting witness and his wife were driving on Highway 35 on their way to a shopping trip in Missoula. The witness was driving, and his wife was napping in the passenger seat. Looking out at Skidoo Bay as he drove, the man saw what he first thought was a wave moving across the water. He quickly realized that there were no boats in sight and that the wind was calm. Realizing he was seeing something unusual, the driver woke his wife so she too could see the creature.

The couple stopped near the top of a hill to get a better look at the object. They observed a large something, moving in a porpoise-like motion and leaving a small wake. As they watched, the creature submerged and vanished from sight.

The reporting witness said the creature was smooth-skinned and very dark in color, black to gray-black. Five humps were visible. The estimated length of the creature was at least twenty feet.

"What we could see of the body led us to surmise that it was long and snakelike—we could make out a round body about 18 inches across at its widest. We determined that circumference by noting that it never showed an underside."

The witnesses estimated that the creature moved between five and eight miles per hour as they watched it move across the lake.

A retired US Army officer has seen something strange in the lake, not just once, but twice.

Major George Cote and his son Neal were on the water on May 25, 1985, trolling for mackinaw trout in Yellow Bay when they spotted a large object surface off the north point of the bay. The Cotes first thought they were seeing SCUBA divers surface, but as they slowly approached the area, they realized it was something else. Whatever it was, it seemed to be chasing large squawfish in the shallows. The Cotes had the impression that the thing raised its head and looked at them as they got closer.

Cote wrote a letter (dated Feb 8, 1990) to *Montana Outdoors* magazine, and his account was included in an article by John Fraley in the November-December 1991 edition of the publication. Cote's letter provided details of the creature they spotted:

"When we got within 60 meters of it, we realized that it was nothing we'd ever seen. The thing was big: as long as a telephone pole and twice as large in diameter. The skin of the creature was smooth and coal black; it had the perfect head of a serpent. There were 4-6 humps sticking out of the water. It moved away from us slowly, then took off like a streak through the water. It stopped about 400 meters out from the bay, looked back, and dove under the waves.

"I asked Neal if he believed what he just saw and he said, 'No, and no one else will believe us either.' So, we didn't say anything until years later."

The Major was lucky because he and his son spotted the monster again two years later. On July 1, 1987, they were near Lakeside on the west shore of the lake when they again spotted the water beast. They watched as the creature changed course twice and estimated its speed at nearly 10 knots. The men had a clear view of the thing's head, body, and tail as it swam toward Caroline point. Cote emphasized his experience with fish and his opinion of the strange animal in his letter to the magazine:

"I've caught bluefin tuna over 1,000 pounds in the ocean. I've seen sturgeon. I've been out on Flathead Lake over 300 times in the last 25 years, and I know what a submerged log looks like. I know what I saw. There's no doubt in my mind that it was a huge creature.

"We're fishermen, and some may think we are stretching the size of this thing, that it's getting bigger in our minds. This is no fish story."

Another Monsterwatch Project report comes from a witness who spotted a creature in the lake in the spring of 1987. The reporting witness was sitting on rocks near the shore with two friends nearby. The trio watched what looked like a giant snake swimming toward the center of the lake. The witness reports that the creature was "about the color of rock—sandstone, and around 30 feet long."

The witness also notes that the creature's skin was smooth, and that it moved like a snake in the water leaving no wake. "The front part of it raised up and looked back toward the shore. The head was sort of like a horse head."

As the group watched, the creature submerged and disappeared.

Highway 93 offers a view of Flathead Lake

Rich Stripp, editor of the *Lake County Leader*, wrote about the monster in his January 16, 1992, "Ramblin Man" column.

Stripp himself saw something in the lake on September 5, 1991, that he couldn't quite explain.

"At about 5:30 p.m., on Sept 5, Libbi (Corbett) and I were motoring along Highway 93 near Ducharme Park when I saw a wake near the shoreline. Something dark was cutting the water pretty quickly, moving west to east. It stuck out of the lake a couple of feet and made a very noticeable wake for 5-10 seconds.

"Libbi saw the same thing and asked me what it was. I told her I didn't know."

An online posting mentions a sighting from May 24, 1993, involving two witnesses at Big Arm Bay who spotted a pair of creatures in the water. One of the animals was large and one smaller, leading to speculation that it was an adult animal with its child. The two creatures were initially swimming together but then split up, taking off across the lake in different directions.

Another pair of sightings from the summer of 1993 has also been posted to numerous sites online.

On July 13, off Woods Bay, a bank officer and a district sales manager on vacation from Seattle were at the lake when they spotted a creature in the water. The pair caught video footage that shows a dark shape, about twelve feet in length, just below the surface of the water. One of the witnesses stated that the thing had a sturgeon-like head and an eel-like body.

Another posting reports that Rich Gaffney, a vacationing police officer, and his family, saw a strange creature surface amidst a school of fish about 50 yards from their boat on July 29, 1993. The man reported that the creature was 15-20 feet in length with a series of humps. The skin was shiny, and the thing's head was about the size of a bowling ball.

A fireman out boating in the summer of 1995 says he saw a giant sturgeon in the water near the southwest corner of Wildhorse Island. The man posted his account on the Monsterwatch Project website, and stated that the sturgeon was between ten and twelve feet in length when it appeared at the back of the boat that he was in.

"The back was all I could see breaking water. The body

appeared to be 14 to 16 inches wide and went on forever…I had never heard of a 'Flathead Lake' monster until later. From what I saw, I feel it was a very large sturgeon that I saw on the surface of the lake."

An October 9, 1996, sighting sent to me (original source unknown), involves a woman named Karen Davis who spotted something odd near Dayton. Davis saw what she first thought was a white capped wave four to five feet in height. She soon realized she was watching an object and not a wave as it moved toward the yacht harbor in Dayton. Davis was positive the object was not a log, but she was unable to make out details. Two other witnesses, Mike Blount, and Victor Davis, also saw the object as it passed by. The area was under pleasant conditions with clear skies and only a gentle wind. There were no boats visible.

James A. Manley and his wife, Julia, appeared on an episode of the *Travel Channel's Monsters and Mysteries in America* to talk about their encounter with the Flathead monster.

The Manleys were at Big Arm Bay on July 28, 2005. James Manley, a Polson trial attorney, says he was enjoying a pleasant afternoon boat ride with his wife when the craft's motor died.

The couple contacted their daughter for help and moored the vessel to wait. They were not far from shore and the calmness was broken by the sound of something large slapping the water's surface. Disturbingly, the sound seemed to be coming toward them.

Julia reported that she felt in "total shock" when she and her husband realized what was producing the sound. The couple saw a serpent-like creature that was as long, and perhaps longer than, their 24-foot boat. Several humps were visible above the water as the creature moved toward them.

At that moment, the Manley's daughter started approaching in another boat and the sound seemed to drive the monster away. It vanished before anyone on the rescue vessel saw it.

Curiously, the same day that the Manleys had their sighting of the water monster, Laney Hanzel received an even more unusual report involving a three-year-old named Andrew Johnson.

Andrew's mother, Cindy, and her sister were busy preparing to take a boat ride on the lake and young Andrew wandered off to the dock by himself. Somehow, Andrew fell into the water. The young boy couldn't swim but what could have been a tragedy turned into an unusual event. Something in the water lifted the boy back onto the dock.

The drenched boy rushed to his mother and informed her that Flessie had saved his life! He added that not only was Flessie there, but she wasn't alone. "She has a baby," Andrew told his mother.

Andrew, now an adult, reportedly rolls his eyes whenever the story is brought up, but his mother points out that "he was serious when he was little." Whatever it was, Cindy Johnson remains thankful that something saved her son that day.

Sightings

MONSTERS OF BIG SKY COUNTRY by David Weatherly

The Monster Today

Today, the Polson Flathead Museum has a display about the Flathead Lake monster, including the mounted sturgeon reportedly caught in the lake in 1955. The museum notes that it may, or may not, be the lake's legendary monster. The museum notes:

"Legend has it that sightings of 'Nessie,' the Flathead Lake version of its own 'monster,' goes back to the earliest days of human habitation in the area.

"'Monster' sightings still occur each year as area residents and visitors spot mystery creatures on the lake surface."

The story of the Flathead Lake monster has been featured on several television programs including the *Travel Channel's Monsters and Mysteries in America* and *Mysteries at the Museum*.

The monster legend has been embraced by locals, and even skeptics can't deny the creature has made its way into local, pop culture. Aside from the display at the Polson museum, the creature's image can be found around town in various depictions. The Cove Deli and Pizza even has a special pizza named after the monster—available in 18-inch size only.

So, prehistoric water monster or giant fish, what lies below the surface of Flathead Lake? There are plenty of people who fall on both sides of the debate.

Tim Shattuck, a Flathead Lake fishing guide, appeared on Destination America's show "Monsters and Mysteries in America," and stated that he had seen the monster himself on two occasions. Shattuck said. "I still believe it's a big old fish."

A man who had fished many years at Flathead Lake told me that he'd never seen a sturgeon in the lake and didn't believe there were any there. "What is in there, is some kind of creature that no one has ever caught," he stated.

The debate continues, and likely will for many years to come. Many hope the monster is caught some day, while others simply enjoy the mystery.

Paul Fugleberg may have the best, final statement on the Flathead Lake monster. He writes:

"Killed, it's gone. Alive, it's a darn good topic of conversation and a superlative tourist attraction. Chances are, it's been in the lake for a good many years, and if it hasn't done any harm in the past, it's a cinch it won't do any harm in the future. So, for once, let's stifle our human impulse to destroy anything we don't understand."

MONSTERS OF BIG SKY COUNTRY by David Weatherly

PART FOUR
Assorted Curiosities

MONSTERS OF BIG SKY COUNTRY by David Weatherly

A Horrible Monster

The June 14, 1895, edition of the *Anaconda Standard*, out of Anaconda, Montana, reported on a mysterious beast that was terrorizing residents along the Teton River, calling it the "Terror of Women and Hens," and noting that it was invulnerable to bullets. The paper reports:

"From time-to-time vague rumors have reached Great Falls of the depredations of a horrible monster which is reported to be roaming at large in Choteau County. Such fear has seized the people along the Teton River that they have made every preparation against the monster, be it man or beast. Women and children are reported to have been frightened by the strange creature to such an extent that they have become seriously ill. Antelope and coyote hunters claim to have seen it skulking along the brush along the Teton, and ranchers claim that at night, hearing disturbances in the sheep pens, they have hastened forth, but just in time to see the brute escaping with a choice mutton clutched in his strange talons

"Many scoff at the stories circulating and profess to believe that the animal is a wolf of great size and unusual courage, but others, more credulous, claim that the animal has avoided bait which would tempt any wolf and say that it is invulnerable to bullets from an ordinary rifle.

"One rancher claims that recently, while his wife was returning from the hen house, about noon, she heard a commotion among the poultry, and returning to the hen house to investigate, as she opened the door a monstrous beast leaped over her head, its hot breath being plainly felt upon her face; and with a sound like a human moan, it disappeared around a building before she had recovered from her fright.

"A lady who was riding along a trail recently saw a queer

beast loping along ahead of her and gave chase to it. She had overtaken it, when it turned and with a cry, more of agony than of terror, rushed past her, frightening her horse so that he threw his rider.

"The *Ford Benton River Press* says of the beast: 'Morgan Williams, who came in from the Teton today, reports there was great excitement in his neighborhood yesterday. A sheep shearer came in on horseback at a breakneck speed, dashing through wire fences and other obstacles, and explained his hurry by declaring that he had been chased over the prairie by a hideous man-eating monster. From the description given of the animal it appeared to be a cross between a mountain lion and a buffalo, its size comparing with that of a 2-year-old heifer.'

"Others declare that the animal is nearer the size of a normal stallion, with the agility of a monkey and the grace of a panther. It is said to have the voice of a human being, but no one has been able to get an accurate description of it."

While the report is vague on details of the creature, it seems that something was on the attack in the region, though most likely, this is a case of exaggeration either by the witnesses, the reporter, or both. The most likely culprit, given the few facts, points to a wolf or mountain lion, though neither is capable of reaching the size of horse.

The Yellowstone Dinosaur

On July 30, 1886, the *Alexandria Gazette*, out of Alexandria, Virginia, had hot news. A monster was spotted near Yellowstone Lake. According to the paper, which announced the story as a "Cinnabar, Montana special to the *Pioneer Press*,"the creature had been seen by multiple witnesses:

"Last Monday a stage driver and two tourists while near Yellowstone Lake claim to have seen an enormous reptile which, while running through the grass, carried its head 10 or 15 feet above ground. They think it must have been at least 30 feet long. A party was organized to pursue the reptile. Yesterday a party of gentlemen, among them Colonel Wear, Superintendent of the Park, and his assistant, Captain Barronette, while near the cave of an extinct geyser in the vicinity of the lake, heard a hissing and saw the head of the reptile thrust out some 15 feet, and immediately withdrawn. Parties are watching for another sight of the monster."

Researcher John LeMay looked into the account for his excellent book *Cowboys and Saurians: Dinosaurs and Prehistoric Beasts as Seen by the Pioneers,* and notes that the names mentioned in the article are those of real figures connected to the history of Yellowstone. He reports that Colonel David W. Wear was superintendent of the park at the time of the report, as well as being a United States senator. He was known to be a "thoroughly honest man" and an active and intelligent superintendent. As for Barronette, LeMay reports:

"Captain Jack Barronette was an early Yellowstone guide who also built and operated the first bridge across the Yellowstone River in 1871. Barronette Peak, located in the park's NE corner, is named for him."

Yellowstone was established as a National Park by

President Ulysses S. Grant in 1872, so the reported incident is early in the park's history.

That two such notable men had their names attached to the appearance of a monster in Yellowstone is, of course, interesting, but as LeMay suggests, we really have no idea whether this would have precluded them from making up a monster sighting to attract tourists to the park.

The initial news report circulated around the country and no doubt caught a lot of people's attention. But further doubt is cast on the veracity of the story by the fact that there was virtually no follow up to the tale. One would assume that if a dinosaur or giant reptile were roaming a national park there would be plenty of people out hoping to capture it.

Rehashing the account a few days later, the August 2, 1886, edition of the *Boston Post* dubbed the creature the "Dragon of Yellowstone Park." The story compared the beast to other reported creatures from the northeast:

"It is difficult to account for the simultaneous appearance of monsters in various parts of the country this year; for, although it is the dull season according to the calendar, fortune has thus far favored the news gatherers, and the summer hotel attractions have not required any fictitious assistance. But, close upon the appearance of the now familiar sea serpent of North Shore, there has followed the capture of a strange creature, part seal and part turtle, in the waters about Block Island, whose description presents stranger points than have ever been conceived with the sea serpent; while from the Yellowstone Park there comes the story of an enormous reptile inhabiting an extinct geyser, which makes excursions through the surrounding wilderness, carrying its head raised to 15 feet above its body by a long neck and hissing as it goes. The sea serpent we know; the Block Island marvel loses something of its strangeness when it is called a 'rubber turtle,' although this designation may not convey a very distinct idea to many minds; but in the Dragon of the Yellowstone Park, we have a novel monster, a resurrected paleosaurus of the distinguished consideration of tourists."

Dragon, dinosaur, or pure fabrication, we simply don't

know what the reality of the creature was, so we're left with another curious anecdote. Whatever the case, there have been no further reports of dinosaurs roaming in Yellowstone Park.

Giant Snakes

Montana has fewer than a dozen species of snake, and of those, the only venomous one is the western rattlesnake. Of course, this does not account for exotic pets kept by residents; and on occasion, pet pythons, boas and other non-native snakes make an escape, but the climate in Montana isn't conducive to the long-term survival of such species.

There are a couple of weird snake stories from the Treasure State that are worth noting here. The first comes from news sources from 1911 when reports claimed that two sheepherders battled a mammoth snake in the Little Pryor Mountains.

According to the January 10, 1911, edition of the *Chickasha Daily Express* of Chickasha, Oklahoma, the snake caused a "great deal of excitement among naturalists and others."

The snake was reported to be taken alive by L.N. O'Dell and J.W. Vaught in a mountain ravine a few miles from the town of Laurel. The men were put on the trail of the serpent after several local natives spread stories about the giant. According to the paper, the reptile was eighteen feet in length, eighteen inches around and weighed two hundred pounds.

O'Dell became interested in stories about the snake and enlisted Vaught to aid in tracking the serpent down. Local guides led the men to the snake's lair but the guides themselves refused to enter the ravine once the party arrived.

The two men discovered a large hole covered with shale rock. Several snake trails were visible around the hole, a clear indication that the reptile was using the spot as a lair. The men cut a square hole several feet away from the entrance and spotted the coils of a giant snake. The commotion roused the snake and the creature started to make a "great noise" and began moving. The snake hunters took the opportunity to grab the beast. As the *Express* reports:

"As the monster started to leave the entrance, O'Dell threw a gunny sack over its head and clasped his arms around its throat. Then one of the weirdest struggles ever recorded in Montana history was on. Back and forth over the narrow ledge the huge snake writhed and twisted, finally tightening itself about O'Dell's hips until he was lifted from the ground.

"Vaught seized the snake by the tail and forced it to release its hold upon O'Dell. The strange contest continued upon the yielding floor of the little ravine for almost three-quarters of an hour before the two men succeeded in tiring the snake, when they bundled it into a sack and took it alive, struggling, to Laurel, as living proof of their strange story.

"The reptile is marked with large, dark mahogany spots, outlined with lighter color, and extending across its back. Its method of killing prey is apparently by constriction, but the spots are not the shape and color of a boa, nor is it an anaconda, as its body is much too large."

O'Dell reported that he believed the snake was not a native of Montana and thought it had come from the Sierra Nevada mountains. Local Native Americans said reports of the creature had been known for at least twenty years.

The specimen was reportedly sent to the Society for the Preservation of Natural History of Montana.

Fast forwarding to the modern era, In October 1978, Eileen Blackburn and her daughter were driving outside of Cascade when they spotted a giant snake. The incident occurred on Highway 15 about two and a half miles outside of town. Blackburn told reporters:

"It was between 20 and 30 feet long and its coils were at least three feet across. It covered my side of the freeway. It was standing, with its head up, and it was taller than the hood of my car. I tried to slow down and I'm sure I hit it, or it struck my car because it hit high on the left-hand side of my car. It appeared to be a sort of gray-white in color with a thin stripe. It had a flat head that came down to a point and the head was wider than the body. The body was about six inches in diameter at its widest point, and, from the way it stood and the shape of its head, it looked like a cobra."

The incident was so shocking that Blackburn almost ran off the road. She was adamant that the snake was not a native animal, stating "I've seen rattlesnakes, bullsnakes, and cobras, and this looked like a cobra."

Cascade Police Chief Earl Damon said that he had received other reports from people who had also spotted the giant. Damon made a search of the area but found no evidence of the serpent. No further accounts surfaced and there's no indication that the rogue serpent was ever captured.

Weird Things in the Big Sky

The prehistoric age was filled with strange and wonderous creatures, many that scientists are still learning about, putting together the pieces of a complex, biological puzzle as best as they can considering the limited evidence.

While the average person is familiar with something as spectacular as a wooly mammoth, there were countless other creatures that roamed the world during the prehistoric age, even giant bugs.

Meganeura were giant dragonflies with wingspans that could reach up to two feet in length. They lived 300 million years ago during the Carboniferous period, so we're talking about a long way from the modern world. But remarkably, one of these long-gone creatures may have been found by a Crow medicine man in the 19th century.

Goes Ahead was a member of the Crow tribe who became a scout for George Armstrong Custer's 7th Cavalry during the campaign against the Sioux and Cheyenne in 1876. The Sioux and Cheyenne were traditional enemies of the Crow Nation and Goes Ahead was one of several Crow scouts employed by the US forces at the time.

Goes Ahead was a survivor of the famous battle of the Little Bighorn and was a witness to Custer's death. His accounts of the battle proved of great value to historians in piecing together a vivid picture of the famous battle.

In 1870, twenty-year-old Goes Ahead went on a vision quest in the Wolf Mountains. During his period of fasting, he saw a strange sight, a winged creature unlike anything he had ever seen before. Alma Snell, the granddaughter of Goes Ahead, related the details of her grandfather's vision quest as it had been told to her by her father and her grandmother, Pretty Shield. Pretty Shield was the wife of Goes Ahead and was, herself, a medicine woman.

In *Fossil Legends of the First Americans*, Adrienne Mayor relates Snell's account of Goes Ahead's vision quest:

"Goes Ahead noticed what he thought was a bird flying very awkwardly, unbalanced, as though the body was too heavy for its wings. It fell twisted at his feet, and he saw that although it had wings, it was not a bird, but more like a serpent—'lizardlike,' said Alma. The body was long and heavy, 'serpentine,' with wings something like a dragonfly's and a tail. Goes Ahead picked up the strange creature, took it home, encased it in beadwork, and wrapped it up. This became his main medicine."

Goes Ahead carried the mummified creature with him everywhere. Some even believe the man's medicine power was instrumental in his survival of the Battle of the Little Bighorn. Some sources say Goes Ahead knew that Custer was going to lose the battle that day.

Whatever the case, after the now famous fight, Goes Ahead went to Squaw Butte, a pine-covered ridge where he climbed high into the treetops and carved the image of his medicine creature into the bark of a tree.

Almost a hundred years later, in 1973, historian William Boyes and Alma Snell traveled to the Little Bighorn battlefield. Boyes knew that Goes Ahead had carved something up in the trees and with Snell's guidance, he sought out the exact location. Boyes located the tree, climbed it, and found the carving left by Goes Ahead. According to the historian, the impression was "a careful carving about 15 to 18 inches long that must have taken hours to make."

Boyes said the carving resembled both a winged serpent and a dragonfly. It's notable that Snell didn't tell Boyes what the creature looked like, so he was under no preconceived notion when he looked for the carving that had been left by the old warrior. Boyes made a sketch of what he found that day and his drawing resembles a dragonfly.

Sadly, the amazing artifact is no longer with us. Goes Ahead kept the preserved creature until 1900, the year that he converted to Christianity. After his baptism, he believed the medicine object was a pagan symbol and disposed of it. Reportedly, either he, or someone close to him, threw the item into the Little Bighorn River where it was lost forever.

Adrienne Mayor notes learning of two other natives who reportedly witnessed strange flying creatures similar to what Goes Ahead saw.

One is Chief Medicine Crow who reportedly saw a "snake with wings" that he drew a sketch of sometime in 1880. The other is a Native American artist named Wayne George whom Mayor met. George reported that during his own vision quest, he had seen both dinosaurs and a Meganeura.

Goes Ahead of the Crow Nation.

Thunderbirds

It should come as no surprise that the sweeping skies of Montana have yielded reports of thunderbirds.

In cryptozoology, the term "thunderbird" has become somewhat generic and is often used for large, flying, bird-like creatures that have been reported by people all over the United States.

In some cases, the descriptions sound like normal birds (other than their incredible size), with feathers, beaks, and other avian features.

In other cases, witnesses report flying creatures that resemble something from prehistoric times with massive heads, long tails, and leathery wings.

Thunderbirds are a puzzling subject. As cryptozoologist Mark A. Hall writes in his book *Thunderbirds: America's Living Legends of Giant Birds*:

"Thunderbirds do not yet have a place in ornithology. But, like many strange animals people report, they will not go away. Thunderbirds have been sustained by American Indian traditions, by a historical and modern record of uncommon claims, and even by physical evidence, most of which has not been preserved for present-day examination."

Some cryptozoologists theorize that thunderbird sightings are the result of witnesses making a mistake in their assessment of the size of the object. Determining the size of something flying in the sky, without any nearby points of reference, can be difficult even for trained observers. Condors, eagles, herons, and other known birds with large wingspans may seem much larger to someone on the ground, especially if the bird is one that is rarely seen.

Of course, scientists don't believe that something as massive as a thunderbird exists, pointing to the relative lack of sightings and photographic or other evidence and noting that with legions of birdwatchers around the country, surely one of them would capture compelling evidence to support the existence of such creatures.

Despite scientific naysayers, thunderbird legends can be found in the traditions of many Native American tribes, and modern accounts do appear.

According to the Kootenai, thunderbirds were once humans and were sinister in nature. Frank B. Linderman mentions the creatures in his book *Kootenai Why Stories: The Authorized Edition* in a passage that cautions people of the thunderbird's powers:

"Old man has painted the leaves and they will soon dance with the north wind. The season when the Thunder-birds visit us has gone. They will come no more until the leaves are green again. They were wicked persons when this world was young. But now they do not make war unless they know that people have spoken against them. It is bad to speak ill of the Thunders. Yes, or even think bad thoughts of them, for thinking bad thoughts is the same as speaking them aloud. And the Thunders hear our thoughts. Remember this."

Beyond folkloric legends, there are accounts of physical sightings of thunderbirds among regional tribes.

Claude Schaeffer recorded several accounts from members of the Blackfoot Nation who reported seeing thunderbirds in Montana in the 19th century. An account of Schaeffer's findings was published in the June 1951 issue of the *Journal of the Washington Academy of Science*, (Vol. 41, No 6).

Schaeffer, a French archeologist, spent time with the South Piegan Blackfoot and learned some of their traditional stories about what the tribe called "Omaxsapitau," meaning "big Pitau" (Pitau being the Blackfoot name for the golden eagle).

In terms of thunderbirds, the earliest account Schaeffer collected came from the 1860s. The account relates a physical sighting and indicates that, like the Kootenai, the tribe also believed thunderbirds were evil in nature.

In the 1860s, a party of Blackfoot, led by Heavy Runner, set out on a horse raid against the Crow tribe. When they reached Bear Creek, they spotted a massive bird flying directly before them. Heavy Runner believed the creature was an ill omen and decided to turn back and abandon the raid. Most of the men agreed with him, but six men ignored the sign and continued. Five of them were killed during the attempted raid, seemingly affirming that the bird was a sign of bad fortune.

In 1879, Mary Jane, the daughter of a Blackfoot named Red Paint, was with her white husband at a summer camp in the Glacier National Park when they spotted four of the giant birds. Two seemed to be juveniles and it appeared the birds were nesting somewhere on Chief Mountain.

Chief Mountain, location of a thunderbird sighting.

Years later, a thunderbird flew over the southern section of the Blackfoot Reservation in 1897. It was spotted by a man named Big Crow and his wife. They said the creature was "immense and dark" with a feathered ruff and bald head.

A man named George Bull Child spotted a thunderbird flying over the reservation in 1908. Several other witnesses were present, including an elder who identified the creature as a thunderbird.

Schaeffer and other researchers believe that sightings of the

California Condor may explain accounts from the Blackfoot and other early peoples of Montana.

The California Condor is a New World vulture and the largest land bird in North America with a wingspan of 9.8 feet. Their plumage is black with patches of white on the undersides of their wings. Their heads are bald and their skin ranges in color from gray to yellow and bright orange.

Condors are scavengers and have a long lifespan, reaching up to sixty years of age in best conditions.

California condors were driven close to extinction due to human elements including poison and hunting. The United States government captured the remaining wild California condors in the late 1980s and began a program to save the birds. In 1991, conservationists started releasing the birds back into the wild.

Sightings of California Condors may explain some thunderbird accounts.

Fossils of condors have been found as far away as Florida

and New York, suggesting that the species was once spread over a very wide range of North America. This could indicate that Shaeffer is correct in his belief that members of the Blackfoot Nation were seeing condors.

Other researchers aren't so sure. After extensive research, Mark Hall came to believe that thunderbird sightings collectively suggested that a rare, large bird unknown to science had lived in North America. Hall further suggested that members of the species may still survive in remote pockets of wilderness.

After collecting numerous eyewitness accounts, Hall concluded that this undiscovered species had several characteristics, including:

- A wingspan measuring 15-25 feet.
- A height of 4-8 feet.
- A head and neck devoid of feathers.
- Dark plumage colored black, brown or gray.
- Feet capable of carrying heavy loads.

Hall wrote that while thunderbirds had an outward appearance like that of a California condor, they were predatory in nature, feeding on large game such as deer, caribou, colts, dogs and, on occasion, humans.

Hall also believed the birds have a long lifespan, are primarily nocturnal, and that they could be migratory.

Fossil records suggest that large, predatory birds, known as "teratorns," likely lived at the same time as early humans. These creatures had wingspans of 12 to 18 feet, so they were massive birds.

These parameters certainly fit the mold of Native American lore and accounts and even modern reports of thunderbirds.

A modern sighting was reported to multiple sources in October 1987 and came from a young man named Matthew O'Brien. Matthew and his father were traveling east in Montana on Interstate 90 when they spotted a giant bird.

The pair was somewhere in the middle of the state when the incident occurred. The bird was flying south to north. O'Brien reports:

"Largest bird I have ever seen, bigger than an eagle or turkey vulture. Estimated wingspan of 15-20 feet. Shaped like a bird of prey. Brief sighting, as we were driving at 60 mph on the freeway. Saw it through the windshield for 10 or 15 seconds before we weren't under it anymore. It was perhaps a few hundred feet up in the air."

My friend and fellow researcher Ken Gerhard chronicled a thunderbird report from early September 1994 involving a 21-year-old man named Tony.

Tony and his younger brother were backpacking near a spot known as Beartooth Plateau, a high elevation range on the state's border with Wyoming. Camping at night near a small lake, they heard a loud splash from something hitting the water. Tony saw something in his peripheral vision.

As Gerhard reports in *Menagerie of Mysterious Beasts*, the creature was quick moving:

"It was moving fast. I reacted by spinning back around and looking up at the same time. What I saw doesn't fit the reality I know. The entire sky full of stars was blacked out as something flew over me. It was a giant silhouette of a birdlike shape. I'm guessing at least ten feet above me but perhaps much more. If that's the case, then the size of it must have been enormous. Twenty-foot wingspan? Thirty feet? I don't know, but it was huge."

Gerhard has spent a lot of time looking into the thunderbird question, and as a result, over the years, he has come across a lot of reports of the creatures. One interesting email he received came in 2015 from a woman who reportedly sees the birds on a regular basis.

The writer, Diane, told Gerhard that her family regularly spots the creatures over their farm, often just before thunderstorms. The property is located in the North Central part of Montana along the Missouri River.

Diane reported that the birds are dark brown to gray in color with a prominent bottom jaw that has a "downward curve." She described the wings as long and relatively slim with a joint where the wings fold. The wingspan, she said, is about fifteen feet. She was unable to say whether the creatures have feathers.

Gerhard includes Diane's description of the flying monsters in his book, *Menagerie of Mysterious Beasts*:

"The legs are not long, nor do they have long tails. The creepy thing about them is they give the impression of being prehistoric, and everyone in our family that has seen them comments on the evil feeling one gets from seeing them, like the hair on the back of one's neck standing up!"

The witness believes the creatures nest in land along the river and at the time of the report, the family had been witnessing the birds for two to three years.

I've talked to a number of people from Montana who report sightings of incredibly large birds in the sky. As stated previously, these accounts are often difficult to consider when there is little point of reference to compare the creature's size. In addition, many of the accounts are simple and brief reports of a massive, winged creature flying overhead.

One interesting account came from a Billings man who told me he was in Glacier National Park in the late spring of 2018 when he observed a massive bird in the sky. The report is interesting because the witness watched the creature land briefly on top of a tree, or at least, attempt to. The man told me that the bird dwarfed the top of the tree when it was near it:

"It was so big that it didn't completely settle on top of the tree, I think it was too big, too heavy to sit up there. I've traveled a lot and I've seen large birds like eagle sitting up on trees. This thing was way, way larger than any bird I've seen in my life."

Thunderbird accounts have long been a puzzle for cryptozoologists. While there is not an abundance of sightings, there are just enough clear and curious accounts to leave one wondering if some undiscovered aerial creature does still exist. If they do, the state of Montana is certainly a likely candidate for their home turf.

163

Montana Mothman

Apparently, thunderbirds are not the only strange things flying around in Big Sky Country. Take the weird, mid-April 1997 account from a witness driving through a heavily wooded area in the western part of the state. The frightening encounter sounds like a classic Mothman sighting.

A winged something with an "ugly gray face" landed on top of the driver's car and started rocking the vehicle violently.

According to the account, published in the *Western Bigfoot Society Newsletter* (#68), the creature pressed so hard against the windshield that it cracked the glass. It rammed the vehicle repeatedly, doing around five hundred dollars' worth of damage, including heavy scratches. Despite the driver racing down the road at 80 mph, presumably in an attempt to shake the thing off, the creature continued to hold on and strike the car for a time before giving up and flying away. The witness notes: "It had red, glowing eyes, was four feet tall, and was brown and gray. It glided along rather than pump the 5-foot-long wings like a bird."

MONSTERS OF BIG SKY COUNTRY by David Weatherly

Attack of the Bird Men

I remember, back in the 1980s, cracking open a new book called *Curious Encounters*, by author Loren Coleman. In it were a range of incredible reports of encounters from around the country, including one particularly bizarre tale involving weird flying creatures who attacked a pair of truckers in Montana.

It was 8:30 in the morning on Monday, October 8, 1984, when a pair of drivers, Robert and Jackie Bair, rushed into the Truckers Inn in Sauk Centre, Minnesota. The Bairs urgently needed to use a telephone—they were under attack!

The couple called authorities for help, then waited. One can only imagine the reaction of the customers and employees at the inn as things unfolded. As details emerged, the Bairs revealed that they weren't being attacked by anything human, but by weird, flying creatures shaped like birds with V-shaped heads—and human feet.

The Travelers Inn, located at the junction of Interstate 94 and Highway 71, was the end point of a chase that had started over 700 miles away. The Bairs reported that the creatures started assaulting them near Billings, Montana, and that the attacks had been ongoing for ten hours. As Loren Coleman recounts:

"It began somewhere near Billings, MT, the couple told Sauk Centre Police Chief George Trierweiler. A bubble-shaped spaceship emerged from a dark cloud and began spraying the Bair's truck with small metal filings. The filings entered the truck's cab and caused a rash on the couple's arms, Robert Bair claimed. Then their truck collied with the spaceship, which had crashed beside the road. A peanut-shaped cylinder tumbled out of the craft, and creatures, which definitely seemed out of this world, humped from the cylinder. The 'aliens' were eight inches tall, bird-like, and very intent on continuing to shoot metal filings at the Bairs. The creatures followed the husband-and-wife team from Billings to Sauk Centre."

According to the Bairs, they had set out for their weekly run, hauling cooking oil from Seattle, Washington, to Madison, Wisconsin. The trip was completely normal until they reached Montana.

At daybreak, the couple spotted some strange objects in the sky, what they described as "nine little ships and one big ship, moving up and down, back and forth in a lurching motion."

The Bairs reported that another man at a Montana rest stop had also witnessed the lights, but there's no record that he ever came forward and the couple apparently did not get any information from him.

Law enforcement was soon on the scene at the Truckers Inn, but they weren't able to bring much clarity to the situation.

While chief Trierweiler was interviewing the couple in the truck stop parking lot, they told the officer that the winged creatures had "guards" perched on nearby streetlights to watch them, "workers" in the trees, and a red-colored "foreman" close by.

Trierweiler scanned the area carefully but could not see the creatures. "They were very scared people, but I did not see what they saw," he said.

The police chief inspected the couple's truck, but found no signs of the reported damage, no scratches on the windshield, and no evidence of the truck being in a collision with anything. He did, however, find metal filings in the vehicle's cab but speculated that perhaps some work had been done in the truck. He also saw red spots on the couple's arms.

Understandably, Trierweiler seemed doubtful about the couple's story, noting that the pair "Went on and on, about drove me nuts."

At the time of the incident, the couple was employed by the Scott Davis Transport Company, a trucking business out of Yakima, Washington. Trierweiler spoke with the Bair's boss at the company. Davis was puzzled over the couple's strange behavior and told the police chief that Bob Bair had worked for him for eighteen years and was one of the company's best drivers.

"They're definitely afraid of something," chief Trierweiler said, exactly what, he couldn't say.

The *Sauk Centre Herald* covered the Bair's bizarre tale in their October 11, 1984, edition under the tongue twisting headline "Trembling Truckers Tell Terrifying Tale." According to the story, written by reporter Roberta Olson, who interviewed the couple, "Killer" Bob Bair wasn't exactly living up to his nickname as he sat drinking coffee and smoking cigarettes. "I'm scared to leave," Bair said. According to the reporter, the look in the man's eyes confirmed just how frightened he was.

The Bairs recounted the full details of their flight from the alien birds, starting with the initial incident involving an unknown craft. The couple said they left their home in Washington for what they assumed would be a routine trip. As Olson reports:

"Things went smooth. They were enjoying the trip, and the shiny three-week old paint job on their semi-trailer boosted their morale. Then they got into Montana.

"A couple of miles ahead they spotted lights. 'We thought it was a plane,' Bob said. The story of their bizarre experiences poured out of them, hands shaking as they drew sketches of creatures, and interrupting each other to agree or expand on a point."

The couple reported that they entered Montana just at daybreak, at which point it became clear to them that the lights were ships of some kind.

As the couple continued their journey, they quickly realized that the ships were following them, and things quickly escalated. Creatures from the ships started attacking the truck. As recounted in the *Herald*:

"The individual things were described as shaped like about eight inch people with V-shaped heads, wings on their backs.

When the things got hostile with the truck and the drivers, they shot fine needle-like shavings like silver metal through the glass of the windshield."

Bob Bair told Olson that the winged creatures were "shaped like a pre-historic bird."

The truckers claimed that the weird creatures went into "attack mode" several times as they raced down the highway. At one stop, the creatures shot out a ray, that Bair described:

"'It was like a backwards tornado' coming from the mouth of the leader of the ships. 'It was like a ray that he was sending down with the funnel. He did it five times, then we left.'"

Jackie Bair claimed that thousands of "little black things... squiggly things" came out of the sky and surrounded the truck. The couple described what looked like Vitamin E capsules forming on the truck's windows. Reportedly, the small objects, or creatures, whatever they were, were small at first then quickly grew to the size of baseballs. Each "capsule" had a "crystal-like thing inside."

The Bairs stopped numerous times on their journey and on each occasion, the bird creatures would also stop and wait for the couple to get back on the road.

Finally, for some unknown reason, the Bairs decided to make their stand in Sauk Centre. The couple refused to travel any further until someone helped them. Their boss in Washington told them to get a hotel room and wait until he could get a replacement driver sent to their location.

After speaking with authorities, the Bairs spent the night at the Travel Host Motel, and on Monday night, Jackie called Roberta Olson to report that strange things were happening in the motel room, including the appearance of metal filings on the beds and the formation of the vitamin E-like capsule things in the shower.

Jackie also reported that when the semi was moved to the motel lot, hundreds of the bird creatures also came and flocked outside. "We knew they would come," Jackie reported.

Both local police and state highway patrol officers were in contact with the Bairs, but no one else could see the winged creatures the couple described. Because of this, Jackie Bair concluded that the things were able to turn invisible.

The couple told Olson that other things were occurring in the motel room while they were holed up, including the appearance of strange writing on Jackie's thigh. All the while, according to Bob Bair, the bird-men continued to lurk outside the motel, firing metal shavings at the couple.

Finally, on Tuesday morning, a relief driver arrived from the S.D.T. company to meet the Bairs and take over the job. Bob rode with the new driver and Jackie followed in a rental car.

The relief driver took the Bairs to Minneapolis, and from there the pair flew back home to Washington, happy to leave Sauk Centre and all the ridicule. "We are accused of being drug addicts and that we're hallucinating. But that's not true," Bob Bair stated.

For her part, Roberta Olson believed that something beyond her understanding was going on with the Bair case. "Something mysterious did happen to those people." She said, "You had to see their eyes." What exactly was unfolding, however, Olson couldn't explain.

Loren Coleman spoke with people in Sauk Centre to get their take on the Bair's tale and he found mixed reactions. Dorothy Sills, manager of the Truckers Inn, was upset because the Bairs tied up the phones once they arrived. She did comment that the couple was dressed well and clean and stressed "They definitely believed what they said they saw was real."

Sills also said the couple frequently ducked as if something was coming at them. She noted that they constantly watched something outside and would shout out, "here comes another one," as they ducked down for cover.

Bob Bair said it was the bird creatures on utility poles outside the diner, and that they were still firing shavings at him and his wife.

But what exactly did the couple see, if anything? Researchers have speculated that the couple could have experienced hallucinations, perhaps from someone spiking their food or drinks with a substance like LSD.

Others postulate that the Bairs inhaled some kind of toxin from the cooking oil they were hauling or from some other source. If this is the case, it seems to be an isolated incident since nothing similar has ever been reported from cooking oil.

In a bizarre, final twist to the story, Bob and Jackie Bair disappeared. Both Loren Coleman and reporter Roberta Olson tried to locate the couple to no avail.

Whatever the case, the story remains a bizarre, unsolved mystery.

Strange things roam Montana's vast landscape.

Living Lights

Tales of ghost lights can be found around the world. Often, the stories are associated with ghostly legends in the area, phantom railroad signalmen or the spirits of others killed on railroad tracks, other tragic deaths and even murders.

In other cases, people attribute ghost lights to fairies or other mysterious creatures. Those of a skeptical mindset quickly claim that the lights are due to normal, explainable things such as the reflection of car lights or the infamous catch all explanation—swamp gas.

Still, some cases are simply baffling from both perspectives and Montana has a couple of cases of strange lights that some profess are beyond explanation.

The May 1974 issue of *Search Magazine* published a letter from a reader who related a personal memory of the state's "purple lights." The writer, E.D. Bufmyer, reports that his experience occurred "some 65 years back," placing the time of the incident around 1909. Bufmyer writes:

"I was in the Bighole Basin of Montana post office, Wisdom. There was a peculiar phenomenon there. This was a manifestation of light about the size of your hand—a beautiful purple color. The outer edge was somewhat darker. This occurred each year about the 21st of June, but few of the inhabitants paid any attention to it—just passed it off as something natural and of no importance.

"No one ever got closer than 6 to 8 feet to one of these lights. They would just float away from in front of you. I witnessed several of these manifestations. There was definitely intelligence connected with these lights.

"These demonstrations lasted about a full moon, then

there were no more of them until the next year. Now, this is the remarkable part. Around there, the rest of the year, horses and dogs could see objects of some kind that man could not see. I recall one time when I was going into Wisdom, riding a saddle horse, the ranch foreman told me to be watchful and not fall asleep because the horse might suddenly spy one of the 'invisible things.' Well, that is just what happened. Coming home again, my horse let out a shrill snort and jumped and almost unloaded me. Then he stood still for a minute and looked around and finally we started on our way home again."

One must wonder what the "invisible things" were thought to be, but sadly, there is no further indication as to what the people in the region thought of the mysterious creatures that lived beyond the sight of human vision.

Wisdom is in Beaverhead County and is still rural, even today. It's about an hour southwest of Butte.

Just over a five-hour drive northeast of Wisdom is another small town with a weird ghost light legend.

Reports from Grass Range, in Fergus County, started cropping up in the 1920s, although, even then, the light had reportedly been manifesting for years prior.

The Grass Range light appeared as a white circle swinging in the night. Because of the way the light moved, many witnesses thought it was someone carrying a lantern across a far field.

Others reported the light being closer to them and in the shape of a large orb. The glow's erratic movements led some to speculate that the light was a drunken man trying to make his way home after a night of revelry. Others speculated that the light was the lantern of a local moonshiner out making late night deliveries. But it soon became apparent that it wasn't a moonshiner or a drunkard and that something odd was afoot.

Those that watched closely noticed that bobbing light would shift in color and shape. Some witnesses reported that the light was no more than a small pinpoint and at a great distance moving in strange patterns.

Homesteaders in the region frequently spotted the light,

sometimes on their own property. Many men grabbed a rifle and took off in pursuit of the glow, thinking it was someone up to no good, but no one was ever able to catch the source of the illumination or even get a glimpse of who, or what, was carrying it.

Numerous men took off in a late-night pursuit of the light, determined to get to the bottom of the mystery, but the pursuits never ended in success.

Many men would report getting close to the light, yet, when they called out, hoping to get a response from the person controlling it, there would be no response.

Stumbling in the darkness, they watched the light stay just out of reach as if taunting them. At times, it would vanish completely, then reappear at a greater distance as if trying to lure the men further and further away from their land.

Some men reported that when they called out to the light, it would shift in color, going from white to yellow to red, then often vanishing completely as if it were somehow responding to their verbal challenge.

Sometimes it seemed as if the light intentionally lured the pursuer out into the wild, then it would disappear, leaving the man standing in the darkness. The lone hunter would be left stranded and have to find his way back in the pitch black or settle in and wait for sunrise.

Despite thorough daylight searches of the area where the light had manifested, no footprints or other evidence to point to a human source was ever found.

It wasn't long before people started to speculate that the light wasn't controlled by a human at all and that the source was something much stranger, perhaps even sinister. Surely, some said, evil forces were at work in the Montana darkness.

The light was said to appear most frequently in the fall, winter, and spring, typically between nine in the evening and midnight. Other witnesses reported it much later in the night.

Some people in the region decided to ignore the manifestation, thinking it best to leave well enough alone and not tempt fate or evil forces. Others took random potshots at the light, hoping to put a stop to the odd phenomenon. Still other residents enjoyed the weird orb, setting up late night picnics and watching for the light's appearance.

Over the years, various theories were put forth to explain the illumination. Some thought the light or lights were the restless spirits of the dead wandering the land. Others believed there was a scientific explanation, perhaps ball lightning, earth lights, or electrical energy. Others pointed to the infamous swamp gas explanation, but they couldn't explain why the gas was appearing where there was no swamp.

Still, some thought a biological source was at play. Perhaps some kind of bioluminescent creature was moving about the fields at night. In later years, some researchers have pointed to UFO related events to explain such weird lights but all in all, no real, solid conclusion has been reached to explain the living lights of Big Sky Country.

The Pryor Mountains, home to a race of little people.

Little People of the Pryor Mountains

The Pryor Mountains are a mountain range that stretches through Carbon and Big Horn counties south of Billings. The range is primarily on the Crow reservation and in the Custer National Forest with portions of them on private land. The mountains are deeply cut by numerous rugged limestone canyons and the south and west slopes rise gradually from the prairie to sub alpine prairie plateaus peaking at over 8700 ft. elevation.

The Pryors are considered a botanical hot spot because of the rich range of plant species found there. Nearly 1000 species of plants have been identified to date, including forty percent of all plant species that grow in Montana and numerous rare and sensitive plants. Wildlife is abundant in the range with bighorn sheep, mule deer, many species of birds, bats and numerous other mammals.

Archeologists date human presence in the mountains from 10-12,000 years ago. The Crow Nation considers the Pryor Mountains sacred, in part, because it is the territory of the little people. According to the Crow, the little people carved the petroglyphs that can be found in the Pryor Mountains.

Although many of the region's tales of little people are centered on the Pryor Mountains, the stories aren't limited to the range or to the Crow tribe specifically. According to the traditions of numerous native peoples in the region, Montana, and some of the surrounding territory was once home to a tribe of powerful little people and some believe the little ones still live in some of the state's sacred places.

The little people are typically described as looking like humans for the most part, with the exception of their small size. Views of the nature of the little people vary by tribe. The Nez

Perce said the little ones lived deep in the woods and could make themselves invisible by rubbing themselves with certain types of grass.

Shoshone lore says the little people were vicious warriors and tricksters. Bad fortune was often blamed on them. If a man suffered an injury, or if his horse went lame, it might be due to the little people and their invisible arrows.

According to the Flathead, the first inhabitants of their territory were a race of dwarfs who stood around three feet tall. They looked like natives, but their skin was very dark.

The Flathead said that the little people owned herds of tiny horses that also stood about three feet in height. Rather than use the animals for riding, the little people used the small horses as a food source during the winter months.

Some of the Flatheads believe the little people were crowded out and pushed high into the mountains before they completely vanished.

The dwarfs were very powerful, and the Flatheads believed that one who obtained a dwarf as his guardian was very fortunate. One person who received such power was a man named Charlie Gabe.

Gabe was a medicine man of the Kalispel tribe who lived on the Flathead reservation. Gabe passed away in the winter of 1936-37, but his power has long been remembered.

Gabe became friends with Harry Holbert Turney-High, an American anthropologist and author. For some unknown reason, Charlie Gabe shared the story of his medicine power with Turney-High. Sharing such a story is rare. Accounts of obtaining spirit power are often deeply personal and many believe that sharing information about the source of one's power weakens it.

Gabe's story is recounted in Ella E. Clark's *Indian Legends from the Northern Rockies*.

According to Gabe, he grew up very poor, living among the Flatheads. When he was fourteen years old, Gabe sought his medicine power. He fasted and climbed high into the mountains to seek a vison. Gabe was a young man who wanted unusual power, so he climbed much higher than most would dare to go. Eventually, he started seeing indications that he was on the right track, signs, and symbols that he understood as indications to continue his trek. Near exhaustion, he found a large hole and peered inside where he saw the little people preparing a dance.

At first, Charlie went unnoticed, but when the little people were finally ready to dance, the chief acknowledged the boy and invited him to come and dance with them. Charlie and the little people danced all night, then slept through the day. This was repeated until they had danced four nights and rested four days. At that point, Charlie knew that his time on the mountain was done. Before he left, he grabbed one of the little people to take back with him. The little man escaped, but Charlie caught him again. This happened again, and again. After the fourth time the young man caught the dwarf, the little man said to him, "You captured me. Well, you must now keep me and feed me for four years. Then you must take me back to my people and free me. When that time comes, I will tell you something good."

For four years, Charlie Gabe kept the little man hidden, feeding him the best food he could find. When the time had passed, he carried the dwarf back up the mountain to his people.

"I have been your guest for four years. From now on when you are in trouble or when you need anything, think hard about me. I will come to your aid. You need not suffer danger anymore. Also, I will give you my power whenever you want to help someone else."

True to his promise, the little man granted Charlie Gabe power and he went on to be a renowned medicine man, revered by both the Kalispels and Flatheads.

Clark's book mentions several tales of the little people. One Flathead reported some of the traditional beliefs:

"In the old days, many dwarfs lived around Rosebud Lake. It used to be surrounded by dense forest with much underbrush. Trees and bushes were so thick that people could get through them only with difficulty. That's the kind of place the dwarfs liked.

"In the evenings, my family would sometimes hear sticks beating against the trunks of trees. My grandparents would say, 'The dwarfs are hitting the trees.' We children would be afraid."

Descriptions of the little people were varied. Some said they wore brown suits and pointed brown caps.

Sasquatch researchers will no doubt note the curious similarities between some of the little people lore and Bigfoot reports. The sagittal crest that is often reported in Bigfoot sightings could, to some, appear to be a hat. Additionally, stories of the little people beating sticks against tree trunks harkens to the reports of Bigfoot "wood knocks," believe to be produced by the creatures striking trees with large pieces of wood.

According to native lore, the little people were able to move up and down trees quickly, and they moved headfirst with their feet on the underside of branches. Despite the odd movement, their caps always remained on their heads. Stories also report that the dwarfs would cry out in the night, a long, continuous wailing sound.

Again, this harkens to Bigfoot accounts and some of the vocalizations the creatures reportedly utilize.

There are, of course, variations in the description of the region's little people. Some sources say the dwarfs were small humans who dressed in all red.

Another type of dwarf in the region were said to be the size of small boys. They lived in cliffs and rocky areas of the mountain, dressed in skins, and carried small bows and arrows. They were said to shout at hunters and lead them astray.

The Shoshone called the little people the Nirumbee and said they often struck at night, killing horses by ripping out their hearts, and stealing children from camps.

During their epic journey in 1804, Lewis and Clark spent time with a band of Sioux on the Vermillion River in what is now modern-day South Dakota. While visiting the tribe, the expedition heard tales of the little people who lived in the region.

Lewis mentioned the creatures in his journal, noting that he was told they were little devils about eighteen inches in height with large heads. According to the Sioux, the little people were constantly alert to any intrusions on their territory. They were capable of firing long arrows with very sharp heads at a great distance. One traditional tale told of a band of 350 warriors who went too close to one of the little people's mounds late one night. The band of warriors were almost completely wiped out, and those that did survive were crippled for life.

The Crow tribe has long had a special relationship with the little people. According to the tribe's lore, the ferocious dwarfs could be dangerous, but could also impart spiritual wisdom and medicine power upon those who were favored.

The little people were also seen as protectors. In the days of intertribal warfare, the little people would ambush war parties of Crow enemies.

The traditional Crow description of the little people differs from other tribes in the region. According to the Crow, the dwarfs are about eighteen inches tall with large, nearly round bellies. They are said to be incredibly strong, but their arms and legs are short. The little people are said to be fierce warriors who feed mainly on meat. Their mouths are full of many sharp, canine-like teeth. The Crow said that the little people made arrowheads out of stone. This has always been a curious bit of information because the Crow themselves made their arrowheads out of bone.

The Crow story of "Lost Boy" mentions a dwarf killing a full-grown elk and carrying it off simply by tossing the animal's head over his shoulder.

The story of Lost Boy, also called Burnt Face, is an interesting tale since it indicates the power of the little people to bestow blessings. It begins when a young Crow boy falls into a bonfire which results in his face being horribly scarred. As a result, he is given the name Burnt Face. Burnt Face stays behind when his people follow the buffalo north. He builds a sun dance lodge and during the ritual, little people appear. They heal the young man's scarred face and tell him where to find his people. They also bless him with healing powers.

The most significant story involving the Crow's interaction with the little people comes from one of the tribe's most famous leaders, Plenty Coups. When the future chief was only nine years old, he learned that his older brother had been killed by Lakota warriors.

Mourning the loss of his brother, the young boy determined that he would need to go on a quest and find the way to avenge his sibling's death. He took a sweat bath and began to fast. Slipping away from the village, he climbed into the nearby hills where he fasted for two more days and nights.

Despite his ritual, he had no vision, so he returned to his people and fell asleep in his father's lodge. On the fourth night, the boy heard a voice in his sleep, telling him that he did not go to the right mountain.

Plenty Coups of the Crow Nation.

As the village prepared to move to the Little Rockies, Plenty Coups prepared himself for a different journey. He climbed near the south side of Two Buttes and prepared his ceremony, burning a root known as e-say, and rubbing his body with sweet sage.

Under the hot sun, the boy walked to the top of the mountain, asking for spiritual help. Receiving no answer, and weak from fasting, and the heat of the sun, the boy finally lay down. When he woke, the stars were out, and he heard his name called from behind him. The voice told Plenty Coups that "they" wanted him, and the boy understood that the spirits wanted to see him. He felt, rather than saw, the guide that had been sent and he stood and walked east until he came to a lodge.

Entering the lodge, Plenty Coup discovered a circle of old warriors, sitting together, counting coup. The lodge was full of powerful warriors and the very forces of nature. They wondered why Plenty Coup had been brought to the lodge and they expressed that the boy did not belong there. Others, however, made room for the young boy to join them. When he sat down, he realized who had welcomed him to sit with them. As recounted in *Plenty-coups, Chief of the Crows:*

"I looked into his eyes. He was a Dwarf-person, chief of the Little People who live in Medicine Rock, which you can almost see from here, and who made the stone arrow points. I now saw that all on my side were the same as he, that all were Dwarfs not tall as my knee."

The dwarf chief demanded that the young boy count coup, (counting coup in this context is the recall of acts of bravery performed by the subject) but the young Crow was well aware that he had not done any great deeds to recall. The dwarf demanded again that the boy place a feather down, and when the young man did so, the dwarf recanted a great deed, one that Plenty Coup would perform in the future.

This was repeated with a second deed, at which point, those in the lodge agreed that no one could do better than the reported deeds. Plenty Coups recalled the words of the dwarf chief:

"He will be a Chief. I can give him nothing. He already possesses the power to become great if he will use it. Let him cultivate his senses, let him use the powers which Ah-badt-dadt-deah has given him, and he will go far. The difference between men grows out of the use, or non-use, of what was given them by Ah-badt-dadt-deah in the first place."

"'Plenty Coups, we, the dwarfs, the Little people, have adopted you and will be your Helpers throughout your life on this world. We have no medicine-bundle for you. They are cumbersome things at best and are often in a warrior's way. Instead, we will offer you advice. Listen!'

"'In you, as in all men, are natural powers. You have a will. Learn to use it. Make it work for you. Sharpen your senses as you sharpen your knife. Remember the wolf smells better than you do because he has learned to depend on his nose. It tells him every secret that winds carry because he uses it all the time, makes it work for him. We can give you nothing. You already possess everything necessary to become great. Use your powers. Make them work for you, and you will become a Chief.'"

When he was still young, Plenty Coups had another experience with the Little People. This time, the young man was in the Crazy Mountains to fast and seek another vision. After ritual cleansing, he waited for a message. After a long process, one of the little people again showed up and led the Crow boy to a vision, one that he learned signaled the disappearance of the buffalo and the presence of cattle.

Plenty Coup's long vision had other messages, too, including information about the tribe's survival and the fact that they would have the land seen from the Medicine Rocks. Today, the Crow Nation is only a short distance from the Pryor Mountains and Medicine Rocks.

Some scholars believe Plenty-coup's vision was profoundly important to the tribe. As noted in the series *Religions of the United States in Practice* (Volume 1) "The Crow people survived the deepest crisis of the nineteenth century in part because of Plenty-coup's vision."

An important site connected to Plenty-coup's vision is now

the Chief Plenty Coups State Park.

In the early 1900s, S.C. Simms gathered some accounts of the Crow tribe's thoughts on the little people and their power. Simms wrote about the tribe for the Columbian museum's Anthropological series (Volume 2, No 5).

Simms's informants told him about a location where barren women would leave baby moccasins, hoping to receive a blessing and be able to bear children. Simms also collected other accounts related to the dwarves:

"They were strong. I heard a woman tell that she had seen tracks like those of children at the mouth of a cave. Afterwards she had a dream in which she was fasting and found animal bones outside. A woman of the size of my granddaughter (nine years old) came out, adopted her, and gave her some medicine. She fasted for four days. After her return, she came to own large tipis and plenty of horses. I have heard another man tell that he had seen tracks near the rock."

Plenty Coups (in center) was a powerful influence on the Crow Nation.

The Pedro Mountain Mummy

Special Note—While the Pedro Mountains are located in Wyoming, I have included the following information about the discovery of a mummy in the range due to the strong connection to little people legends in Montana.

In 1932, Cecil Main and Frank Carr were looking for gold. They had been working a rich vein in the San Pedro Mountains sixty miles from Casper, Wyoming, but they kept running into more and more rock, making it difficult to extract the valuable ore. Finally, they used dynamite to blast a section of the mountainside, hoping to get to more gold. As the dust of their blast settled, a cave came into view. The small cavern was about fifteen feet long and four feet high. The men had no idea the cave was there until the blast revealed the opening. The entrance had been completely sealed from the outside world, but the dynamite had opened it enough that they could enter.

Inside, they made an amazing discovery. Sitting on a rock ledge was a mummy. The figure was human, and in a cross-legged sitting position, its hands folded in its lap. Seated, it was only about 6 ½ inches tall and it was estimated that the standing height of the figure would have been about 14 inches.

The figure's skin was brown and wrinkled, and the face appeared to be that of an old man. The forehead was low and flat, the eyes were heavy-lidded, the nose flat, and the mouth wide with thin lips.

The mummy was so well preserved that its fingernails could still be seen on its hands. The top of the figure's head was covered in a dark, jelly-like substance that was still pliable.

Was this a mummy of one of the region's famous dwarfs?

The prospectors took the mummy to Casper where it

caused quite a stir. Scientists from all over came to study the find and speculations ran rampant.

Experts initially thought the mummy was a hoax, but others were not so sure. X-rays were done and showed that the mummy had a human skeleton. A careful study of the body also revealed that the being, whatever it was, had met a violent end. The spine was damaged, the collarbone broken, and the skull had been smashed in by a heavy blow to the head. The soft substance on the head was determined to be congealed blood and exposed brain tissue.

Another odd finding was that the mummy had a full set of canines and that the teeth were overly pointed. Again, this harkened to traditional stories of the region's little people and their mouths of sharp teeth.

After the test results were in, scientists stated that the mummy was that of a full-grown adult, approximately 65 years of age at the time of his death.

As with any such find, there was controversy. Allegedly, the tests were performed by the American Museum of Natural History and further certified as genuine by Harvard University's Department of Anthropology.

Alternate reports claim that the mummy was later examined by the University of Wyoming where it was determined that the body was that of a child.

For years, the mummy was displayed in sideshows. It was purchased by a Casper, Wyoming, businessman named Ivan T. Goodman who reportedly kept it on display in his store window. Some sources indicate that it was Goodman who took the mummy for examination and X-rays. According to Lawrence and Ober in *Montana Myths and Legends*, the examination was performed by Dr. Harry Shapiro of the American Museum of Natural History in New York City.

The same book reports that Dr. George Gill, an anthropology professor with the University of Wyoming, received the X-Rays and concluded that the mummy was that of an infant or fetus.

The more skeptical minded embrace Gill's proclamation

that the mummy was merely a human child rather than something more unusual, but it should be noted that by all indications, Gill only studied the X-Rays and not the mummy itself.

When Ivan Goodman passed away in 1950, the mummy was purchased by a New York businessman named Leonard Walder. When Walder died in the 1980s, the mummy vanished.

Legend says that the mummy brought bad luck to those who possessed it, though there are no tales that elaborate on this claim. Main and Carr, the prospectors who first found the mummy and brought it to the world's attention, never had any real luck with their mining operations. They registered the claim in Carbon County and dubbed it "Little Man Mine," but it never really produced much gold. Today, a sign in the Shirley Basin signifies the location of the old mine.

MONSTERS OF BIG SKY COUNTRY by David Weatherly

Modern Accounts of the Little People

Shirley Smith had a long fascination with the region's little people. For forty years, Smith owned the Little Cowboy Bar and Museum in Fromberg, MT. Smith sold the business in 2012 and sadly, it was lost in a fire in December 2013.

The bar and museum gained quite a reputation in its time. In 2007, it was named Montana's best bar by Esquire magazine and the museum side had thousands of items from the region's history.

During her time running the business, Smith would readily discuss tales of the little people with patrons, and she collected many stories and anecdotes about the dwarves.

Amid the historical documents Smith found was an account of two cowboys who, after being on the trail for several days, settled in around a campfire for the night. One of the men woke late in the night to check on the fire and discovered that he and his companion were surrounded by a band of people. To his shock, they were no more than three feet tall.

Other people tell tales of going into the Pryor Mountains and finding campsites ready, complete with campfires going but no one around. Smith herself had such an experience when she and four other people went to picnic on the lower edge of the Pryor Mountains. It was a sunny, summer day and they arrived at their designated picnic site around noon. To everyone's surprise, they found a freshly constructed fire waiting for them, not something normal for the middle of a sunny day, but there was no one else in sight.

Smith recalls seeing the famous mummy when she was seven years old, but it's not the only mummy story she has. She reports that an uncle who ranches around the Pryor Mountains discovered another burial site connected to the little people. The man was digging an irrigation ditch with his tractor when a section of dirt collapsed, revealing a large cave. He retrieved a lantern and returned to the site to investigate. He peered inside and discovered that three sides of the cave were filled with dirt shelves lined with the petrified mummies of little people.

Rather than report the find, the man covered the cave entrance and has refused to disclose its location to anyone, choosing instead to respect the spot as a sacred burial site.

In 1991, two members of the Crow tribe shared a story with Rich Pittsley, former manager of Plenty Coups State Park.

The pair were reportedly surveying a shallow cave in an area near the reservation when one woman took a break for lunch. She sat down near a cave entrance and suddenly a little man appeared. He was about three feet tall, powerfully built and dressed in old fashioned, traditional animal hide clothing.

The little man vanished, and the woman and her friend decided to say a prayer and leave an offering of food at the location.

Some sightings of the little people are quite strange. In 1998, a Crow woman reported that she saw a little man along a two-lane road on the reservation. The little man was pushing a wheelbarrow as he strolled along the road, but stranger still, he was wearing what the woman described as an "Elvis Presley" style outfit!

Initially, she thought she was so tired that she was hallucinating, but later the same day, her sister described seeing the same little man while on the same road.

Further confirmation came when the women shared their sighting with others and found out that a local farmer was frustrated because his wheelbarrows had disappeared.

A thread about the little people of the Pryor Mountains on the Unexplained Mysteries forum had an interesting post in 2016. A user going under the forum name "The Paranormal Site" recounts a story he heard while growing up on the Crow reservation. The poster recounts a story told by his father involving a tribal medicine man and his interactions with the little people:

"This medicine man would stay up on the buffalo pasture through the winter and keep an eye on the herd. He was an absolute believer in the little people and said he used to trade with them when he was snowed in at the cabin by the pasture. He said that he would keep packages of tobacco on hand and when he was low on food, he would leave a package of tobacco on the front deck of the cabin. In the morning, the package would be gone and in its place would be a freshly killed deer."

Reportedly, the man finally got curious about the little people and what they looked like, so he decided to stay awake and watch them make the trade. He put a pouch of tobacco out to trade and waited. He saw a single little man haul a deer up to the porch and drop it off.

"He said the moon was full, so he got a fairly good look at the being that was a perfectly proportioned, heavily muscled man, around 2 feet tall, but an overly large head that had a large nose and a mouth full of sharp teeth."

The poster notes that his father had likely heard the story sometime in the mid-1950s, and that the man's trades with the little people were probably sometime between the 1930s and 1950s.

I received a report from a Montana resident who told me she had seen a little person while hiking in Montana in 2016.

The woman and a younger male friend were on a day hike on a beautiful late spring day when they spotted what she describes as a "little man."

"We were climbing up the trail and had just stopped for a brief break and some water. My hiking companion that day was a younger relative, and he wasn't used to hiking much. He was sitting on a rock and I had just passed him a water bottle when I heard a noise from up to my right. I looked up into the rocks, expecting to see an animal, but it wasn't an animal, it was a small man maybe a couple of feet tall."

The witness told me the little man stood there looking

down at them for a few seconds, then turned and walked across the rocks and was quickly out of view.

"He was almost like a garden gnome, but his clothes were not brightly colored. He was dressed in a button shirt and pants with boots on. He had a red hat, but it was dull red in color and it was short, not tall like you typically see in gnome drawings.

"I just don't know what to think. I wasn't tired or hallucinating from heat or exhaustion and my nephew saw the little man, too. I know what I saw."

Do the mountains of Montana still hide a race of dwarfs? While it may seem unlikely to many people in the modern world, modern sightings are, at the least, puzzling, and leave one wondering exactly what mysteries we may still uncover in the years to come.

Modern Accounts of the Little People

MONSTERS OF BIG SKY COUNTRY by David Weatherly

Acknowledgements

A Special thanks to John LeMay for the great foreword and some research notes. Thanks to Karen Dunwell and the Polson Flathead Historical Museum for valuable information regarding the Flathead Lake Monster and Ken Gerhard for sharing some of his research findings on the creature. And of course, thanks to Mister Sam Shearon for continuing to provide amazing covers for this series.

As always, I am grateful for the support of my friends and colleagues as this series of state cryptid books continues to unfold. Lyle Blackburn, Loren Coleman, Dr. Jeff Meldrum, Chad Lewis, Kevin Nelson, Nick Redfern, Joshua P. Warren, Micah Hanks and others continue to provide valuable input.

And as always, thanks to all the witnesses and organizations who have shared their sightings, opinions, and information.

MONSTERS OF BIG SKY COUNTRY by David Weatherly

Bibliography

Baumler, Ellen. Beyond Spirit Tailings: Montana's Mysteries, Ghosts, and Haunted Places. Montana Historical Society Press, Helena, MT 2005.

Bord, Janet & Bord, Colin. Alien Animals: A Worldwide Investigation—Lake Monsters, Giant Birds & Birdmen, Black dogs, Mystery pumas, Bigfoot. Stackpole Books, Mechanicsburg, PA 1981.

Clark, Ella E. Indian Legends of the Northern Rockies. University of Oklahoma Press, Norman, OK 1966.

Coleman, Loren. Curious Encounters. Faber and Faber, Inc., Winchester, MA 1985.

Coleman, Loren. Mysterious America. Faber and Faber, Inc., Winchester, MA 1989.

Coleman, Loren & Clark, Jerome. Cryptozoology A to Z: The Encyclopedia of Loch Monsters, Sasquatch, Chupacabras, and Other Authentic Mysteries of Nature. Fireside/Simon & Schuster, New York, NY 1999.

Crowe, Ray. Bigfoot Behavior Volume II. Createspace Independent Publishing, 2015.

Crowe, Ray. Bigfoot Behavior Volume III. Createspace Independent Publishing, 2015.

Cutchin, Joshua, and Renner, Timothy. Where the Footprints End Volume 2: Evidence. Independently published 2020.

Donovan, Roberta, and Wolverton, Keith. Mystery Stalks the Prairie. T.H.A.R. Institute, Raynesford, MT 1976.

Fugleberg, Paul. Montana Nessie of Flathead Lake. Treasure State Publishing company, Polson, MT 1992.

Gerhard, Ken. A Menagerie of Mysterious Beasts. Llewellyn Publications, Woodbury, MN 2016.

Green, John. Sasquatch: The Apes Among Us. Hancock House Publishers, Surrey, British Columbia 2006.

Hall, Mark A. Thunderbirds America's Living Legends of Giant Birds. Paraview Press, New York, NY 2004.

Hutchins, Ross. Trails to Nature's Mysteries: The Life of a Working Naturalist. Dodd, Mead & Co. Publishing, New York, NY 1977.

Kern John D., and Griggs, Irwin. This America Reprint Edition. Kessinger Publishing, LLC., Whitefish, MT 2010.

Lawrence, Ed, and Ober, Michael. Montana Myths & Legends. Twodot, Helena, MT 2016.

LeMay, John. Cowboys and Saurians: Dinosaurs and Prehistoric Beasts as Seen by the Pioneers. Roswell Books, Roswell, NM 2019.

Linderman, Frank B. Kootenai Why Stories the Authorized Edition. Bison Books/University of Nebraska Press, Lincoln, NB 1997.

Linderman, Frank B. Plenty-coups: Chief of the Crows. Second edition, Bison Books/University of Nebraska Press, Lincoln, NB 2002.

Lowie, Robert H. Myths and Traditions of the Crow Indians. Bison Books/University of Nebraska Press, Lincoln, NB 1993.

Matthiessen, Peter. In the Spirit of Crazy Horse. Viking Press, New York, NY 1991.

Mayor, Adrienne. Fossil Legends of the First Americans. Princeton University Press, Princeton, NJ 2007.

McDannell, Colleen, editor. Religions of the United States in Practice, Volume 1. Princeton University Press, Princeton, NJ 2001.

Place, Marian T. Bigfoot All Over the Country. Dodd Mead Publishing, New York, NY 1978.

Roosevelt, Theodore. The Wilderness Hunter—An Account

of the Big Game of the United states and Its Chase with Horse, Hound and Rifle. G.P. Putnam's Sons, New York, NY 1893.

Sanderson, Ivan. Things. Pyramid Books, New York, NY 1967.

Skinner, Alanson. Ethnology of the Ioway Indians: Bulletin of the Public Museum of the City of Milwaukee V 5, No 4. 1926.

Thorning, Ruth. What's in a Bitterroot Place Name. Bitterroot Star, Stevensville, MT.

Weatherly, David. Silver State Monsters: Cryptids & Legends of Nevada. Eerie Lights Publishing, 2019.

Wheeler, Olin D. The Trail of Lewis and Clark 1804-1904 Vol 1 and 2. G.P. Putnam's Sons, New York, NY 1904

Wherry, Joseph H. Indian Mask & Myths of the West. Funk & Wagnalls, New York, NY 1969.

Magazines & Journals

Anomaly Research Bulletin

Columbian museum's Anthropological series (Volume 2, No 5), Chicago 1903

Journal of the Washington Academy of Science June 1951

Montana Sports Outdoors December 1960, July 1969, Nov-Dec 1991

Saga magazine January 1961, July 1969

Search May 1974

Western Bigfoot Society Newsletter

Websites

BFRO.net

Bigfootencounters.com

Cryptozoo-oscity.blogspot.com

MonsterWatch Project

Oregonbigfoot.com

Paranormal Montana

Unexplained-Mysteries.com

Bibliography

About the Author

David Weatherly

David Weatherly is a renaissance man of the strange and supernatural. He has traveled the world in pursuit of ghosts, cryptids, UFOs, magic, and more. From the specters of dusty castles, to remote, haunted islands, from ancient sites, to modern mysteries, he has journeyed to the most unusual places on the globe seeking the unknown.

David became fascinated with the paranormal at a young age. Ghost stories and accounts of weird creatures and UFOs led him to discover many of his early influences. Writers such as John Keel, Jacques Vallee, Hans Holzer and others set him on course to spend his life exploring and investigating the unexplained.

Throughout his life, he's also delved into shamanic and magical traditions from around the world, spending time with elders from numerous cultures in Europe, the Americas, Africa and Asia. He has studied with Taoist masters in China, Tibetan Lamas, and other mystics from the far east. He's picked up knowledge from African and Native American tribal elders and sat around fires with shamans from countless other traditions.

Along his path, David has also gathered a lot of arcane knowledge, studying a range of ancient arts from palmistry, the runes, and other obscure forms of divination, to alchemy and magick. He has studied and taught Qigong and Ninjutsu, as well as various energy related arts. David has also studied stage and performance magic.

His shamanic and magical background has given him a unique perspective in his explorations into the unknown, and he continues to write, travel, and explore, leaving no stone unturned in his quest for the strange and unusual.

David has investigated, and written about, a diverse range of topics including, Hauntings & Ghosts, Cryptozoology, Ufology, Ancient Mysteries, Shamanism, Magic, and Psychic Phenomena.

David is the founder of the independent media and publishing company, Eerie Lights Publishing.

He has been a featured speaker at conferences around the world and has lectured for countless paranormal and spiritual groups.

He is a frequent guest on Coast to Coast AM with George Noory, Spaced Out Radio and other radio programs. David has also appeared on numerous television shows including the Travel Channel's Mysteries of the Outdoors, History Channel's Ancient Aliens, Beyond Belief and other programs. He was also featured in the highly successful series On the Trail of UFOs.

David's books include Strange Intruders, Eerie Companions, and the Monsters of America series.

Find David online at:

https://eerielights.com